Arizona, Utah & New Mexico

A Guide To The State & National Parks

Barbara Sinotte

HUNTER
PUBLISHING

Hunter Publishing, Inc.
300 Raritan Center Parkway
Edison NJ 08818, USA
Tel (908) 225 1900
Fax (908) 417 0482

ISBN 1-55650-739-9

Maps by Kim André

Cover photo by David G. Houser

Other titles in the Parks Series include:

CALIFORNIA, COLORADO, NEW ENGLAND, NEW YORK &

NEW JERSEY, OREGON & WASHINGTON

Contents

A Word About Hiking...

ARIZONA

UTAH

Maps

A Word About Hiking...

$\mathcal{H}$iking is by far the most popular activity in state and national parks. Most of the hiking involves following clearly marked trails. Off-trail travel (commonly referred to as bushwhacking) is practiced by the more adventurous hikers – especially in the clearer, less-populated areas of the parks.

Trails in many state parks have been rated according to distance and degree of difficulty. If you are not sure which trails are appropriate for you and your family, talk to a park ranger. If you do not exercise regularly, start on beginner trails and increase your distances gradually. Trail maps are usually available either at the trailhead or at the ranger station.

While trail markings vary widely, there are a few common indicators that everyone should be familiar with. Periodic paint blazes on trees or rocks are clearly the most popular method of marking a trail. Plastic markers are often nailed to trees or metal signs are mounted on their own wooden posts. Where there are no trees, trails may be marked with piles of rocks.

If you want to go bushwhacking, be careful. Make your first attempts in open areas with limited undergrowth, such as a desert area where the terrain is a little easier to tackle. Bushwhacking through areas of dense vegetation is for the more experienced hiker and should only be attempted with map, water and compass in hand.

Whether you are bushwhacking or following designated trails, set a pace that will make the experience enjoyable for you. You are not in a race and can better take in the surroundings if you are walking at a comfortable speed. Remember that going too fast can ruin all the fun and burn you out. Stumbling or tripping is a clear sign that you need to slow down.

Take frequent rest stops. Don't wait for fatigue to tell you it's time to slow down. A 10- to 15-minute stop every hour or so is a good idea to begin with. After a while you will know what is best for you.

Don't speed over the rough areas of a trail. Watch out for tree roots and old logs that may be damp and slippery. If you are uncertain as to your footing it is wise to crouch; lowering your center of gravity will reduce the likelihood of falling. Steep trails have caused more than one hiker to lose their balance and take a tumble. Descending tends to be more hazardous than ascending and requires a little more attention. Hold on to small trees or rocks to balance yourself. When in doubt, sitting and easing your way down on your rear might just be the way to go.

It is important to choose a trail that is comfortable for everyone. Younger children should be introduced to hiking with short walks. It is more fun and educational if they can be involved in planning the hike.

Checklist for a Day Hike

2 pairs of hiking socks
Liner socks
Long pants
Long-sleeved shirt
Shell parka or windbreaker
Toilet Paper
Plastic litter bag
Trail guidebook
First aid kit
Pocket knife

Hiking boots
Day pack
Water bottle
Waterproof poncho
Extra sweater
Snack foods
Map
Compass
Flashlight
Matches

In warm weather add:
T-shirt
Shorts
Extra water
Bug repellent
Sunscreen
Sun hat

In cold weather add:
Additional layers
Cap or hat
Thermal underwear

Hiking Safety

- Hike with a friend.
- Take plenty of drinking water.
- Let someone at the camp or at home know where you are going and when you plan to return.
- Don't take shortcuts on switchback trails.

Arizona

State Parks

Arizona State Parks system has 24 natural, cultural and recreational parks currently open to the public. Two parks, Kartchner Caverns and Oracle, are being developed and will not be open for a few years. The natural and recreational parks are open year-round, while the historic parks have normal business hours and are closed on Christmas Day.

McFarland is closed on Tuesday and Wednesday. Slide Rock, Tonto National Bridge and Red Rock have no camping facilities.

Camping & Hiking

Most of Arizona's natural and cultural parks are dotted with campsites and laced by trails. The roads leading to the parks usually have a commercial campsite for RVs, complete with cable TV.

A word to the wise: Be sure to reach your campground early, especially during the late spring and fall months. Sites are available

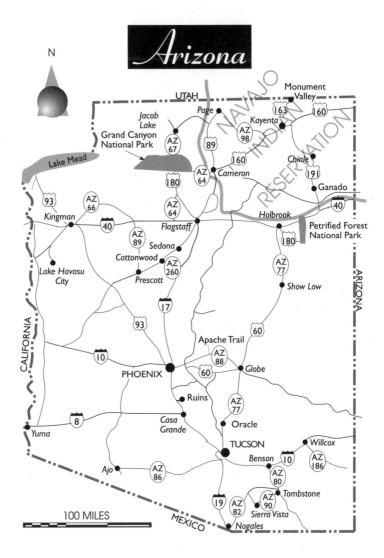

for a small fee on a first-come, first-served basis. Developed sites usually include running water, restrooms, and RV hook-ups.

Hikers can choose from trails that wind through desert, head over mountains, venture deep into forests or meander around city perimeters. There are many miles of marked paths challenging even the most experienced hiker.

On the trail, be sure to carry plenty of water. Note that backcountry hikers might meet poisonous snakes face to face. Be alert! Check with the local governing agency to see whether fires are permitted in the area you are planning to visit. Never venture out without a good map, which you can pick up at the park office.

Read the Hiking section at the beginning of this book for proper conduct, safety tips, and general rules to be observed while in the backcountry.

Biking

Despite the hot Arizona sun, bicycling is a popular sport through-out the state. Desert trails, mountain passes and the open road call cyclists to the challenge. Experts will caution you to begin your trip with plenty of water, cool clothing, plenty of sun screen and, of course, a lightweight touring bike. For specific information on bike paths in the Phoenix area, contact the **Maricopa County Parks Recreation Department.** ☎ (602) 272-8871.

Fishing

Don't be surprised as fish jump out of cool mountain streams and man-made lakes – Arizona is a fisherman's dream. Rainbow, brown, brook, and cut-throat trout test the skills of anglers, along with catfish, crappie, bass, pike and bluegill. **Tip:** Hunt for a spot on San Carlos Lake for the best bass fishing.

Hunting

Take your choice from elk, deer, bear, mountain lion, buffalo, tur-key, quail, antelope, goose and rabbit. Make sure to obtain the required permits from the **Arizona Game and Fish Department** at 2221 W Greenway Road, Phoenix, AZ 85023, ☎ (602) 942-3000. They will also give you information about hunting seasons and a map of permitted areas.

River Rafting

Rafting and kayaking trips down the Colorado River and through parts of the Grand Canyon are popular with visitors and locals alike. Challenging one-day to two-week trips are offered during the summer. The Arizona Dept. of Tourism has a current list of operators (see below).

Canoeing

The most popular canoe trip that provides swift currents without the dangers of rapids is the day-long Topock Gorge excursion on the Colorado River. Beginning at Topock, canoeists travel through a picturesque wildlife refuge to Castle Rock at the top end of Lake Havasu. Canoe rentals are readily available.

Want to Know More?

If you need more information on any of the parks throughout the state, contact:

Arizona State Parks
800 W Washington
Phoenix, AZ 85007
(602) 542-4174

Alamo Lake State Park

Location: Northwest of Wickenburg, near Wendon, off Highway 60.
Access is via 38 miles of paved road.

An oasis for anglers and nature lovers, Alamo Lake State Park offers classic Sonoran Desert scenery and the promise of uncrowded views. Principally a flood control reservoir, the park is located on the Bill Williams River, about 30 miles before it enters the Colorado River. It sits in the heart of one of Arizona's wide-open spaces: the unspoiled Bill Williams River Valley. Although the lake's water level fluctuates significantly, the water teems with largemouth bass and catfish. An abundance of outdoor activities includes wildlife watching and hiking against a backdrop of the picturesque Rawhide and Buckskin mountains.

For those who want to get away from it all, Alamo Lake State Park offers unparalleled advantages in relaxation, clean air and quiet. Overnight guests have a choice of undeveloped or developed campsites, or complete hookups with water, sewer, and electricity. Showers, a dump station, and boat launching facilities are also available. A store in the park offers fishing tackle, live bait, lures, rental boats, ice, and camping supplies (no gasoline or propane).

For nature lovers, there are plenty of wildflowers in the spring, and many species of birds to admire, including waterfowl. The bald and golden eagle are frequently seen around the lake. Other wildlife frequently seen in the area includes fox, coyote, mule and deer. The park is also known for its resident wild burro.

Alamo Lake was formed by the construction of a dam on the Bill Williams River by the US Army Corps of Engineers. Construction of the dam began in 1964 and was completed in 1968. The park and recreational facilities were dedicated in November, 1969.

The Bill Williams River is formed where the Santa Maria River and the Big Sandy River come together at the upper end of the lake. These rivers have a drainage area of 4,770 square miles. Heavy run-off from rain storms in the drainage area has caused the lake to rise as much as 100 feet – 11 feet have been gained overnight. The maintained recreation pool of 3,000 to 4,000 surface acres has created one of the best warm-water fisheries in the Southwest for bass, bluegill, and catfish.

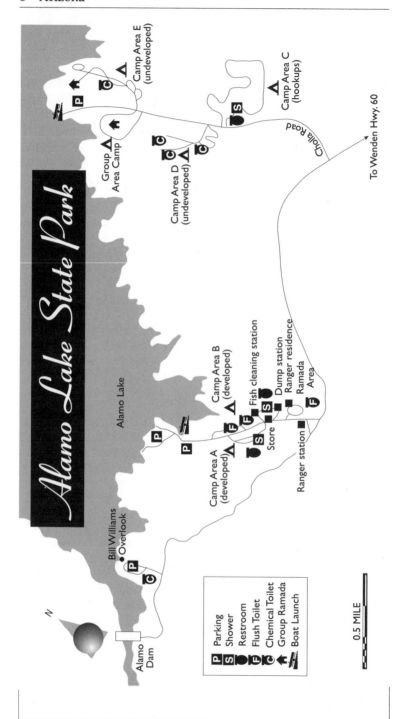

Alamo Lake State Park

Alamo Lake

Bill Williams
Overlook

Alamo Dam

N

Camp Area E
(undeveloped)

Camp Area C
(hookups)

Group
Area Camp

Camp Area D
(undeveloped)

Cholla Road

To Wenden Hwy. 60

Camp Area B
(developed)

Fish cleaning station

Dump station

Ranger residence

Ramada
Area

Store

Camp Area A
(developed)

Ranger station

P   Parking
S   Shower
◑   Restroom
F   Flush Toilet
C   Chemical Toilet
🚻   Group Ramada
⚓   Boat Launch

0.5 MILE

A word of caution: The desert can be harsh and dangerous, but it is also very fragile. Help protect it, and yourself, by camping in designated areas, and by keeping your vehicles on maintained roadways.

For further information contact the Park Superintendent, Alamo Lake State Park, PO Box 38, Wenden, AZ 85357. ☎ (602) 669-2088.

Boyce Thompson Southwestern Arboretum

Location: East of Phoenix, 3 miles west of Superior along Highway 60.

The arboretum is cooperatively managed by the University of Arizona and the Boyce Thompson Arboretum Board. It was established in the early 1920's by botanical enthusiast William Boyce Thompson. While growing into a major center for plant research, it has also blossomed into a lush desert garden. Arid-region plants and trees from around the world line scenic walks through the garden's 35 acres. The arboretum's shaded picnic area is ideal for a leisurely lunch.

Visit anytime and many times. There is always something new to see, to learn, and to enjoy. Walk the shaded paths in summer. In fall, see red and golden autumn leaves, colorful fruits and berries. Warm winter sun brings blooms to many of the strange and marvelous succulent plants from other lands. Spring bursts in with a profusion of cacti and flowers in the gardens and greenhouses. The plants are studied in many ways: for drought-tolerance, usefulness to man, landscaping potential, and their place in the ecosystem.

Begin your visit at the Visitor Center. On the National Register of Historic Sites, this picturesque building houses displays, an information center, and the Arboretum gift shop, containing a fine bookstore. Numerous species of unusual cacti, succulents and water-efficient trees and shrubs are for sale. Two adjacent glass houses erected in 1924 exhibit collections of cacti and other succulents.

Nature trails wind through 35 acres of grounds, sampling the many lovely plantings and vistas. Wildlife abounds. A shaded picnic area invites leisurely lunching. Arboretum special events, interpretive displays, lecture series and workshops are scheduled throughout the year.

Experience a year-round garden of many delights. See a veritable Noah's Ark of desert plants. Walk beneath majestic shade trees and between soaring canyon walls. Listen to the murmur of Queen Creek and the songs of many birds. Smell the clean air, the fragrant flowers, dry leaves under foot. Relax. Escape. Enjoy!

For further information contact the Superintendent, Boyce Thompson Southwestern Arboretum, 37615 E. Highway 60, Superior, AZ 85273. ☎ (602) 689-2811.

Buckskin Mountain State Park

Location: The park and its associated River Island Unit are approximately 11 miles north of Parker off Highway 95.

*N*estled against the Buckskin Mountain range and situated along the lower Colorado River at an elevation of 640 feet, Buckskin Mountain State Park is located in a dramatically scenic region of the Mohave Desert. The Buckskin range is home to the reclusive desert bighorn sheep. Hikers are enticed to explore the area via three developed trails that ascend steep bluffs to panoramic overlooks. The river attracts boaters, water skiers, and swimmers to this recreation area. Anglers vie for largemouth bass, crappie, channel catfish, and bluegill. A level fishing pad is provided for wheelchair access.

The seemingly desolate landscape hosts an abundance of life forms adapted to extreme heat, including such plant life as cholla, saguaro, barrel cacti, palo verde and creosote. A short-lived spring bursts forth with a dazzling display of desert wildflowers, including gold and orange California poppies, before quickly fading to searing summer. Coyotes and jack rabbits engage in an age-old conflict where survival is the prize.

The park campground provides lawn and shade, beach areas, and other amenities, offering a welcome contrast to the surrounding environment. A mild winter climate brings myriad recreational opportunities for visitors, including camping, hiking, fishing, and birdwatching. During the summer months, water sports reign;

waterskiing, tubing, fishing, and boating on the Colorado River. Day trips to the London Bridge, Colorado River Indian Tribe Museum, and Parker Dam may be enjoyed year-round.

Buckskin Mountain Scenic Trail (2½ miles), Lightning Bolt Trail (a half-mile), and Wedge Hill Trail (a quarter-mile at the River Island Unit) provide panoramic views of the Colorado River Valley. Hikers will see desert habitat and old prospecting claims.

Keep in mind: Temperatures can be extreme, often exceeding 110°F in summer. Avoid overexertion and overexposure to the sun. Carry ample water and travel with a companion. Rhyolite rock cliffs are unstable and not safe to climb. Swim at your own risk; no lifeguards are on duty. Observe laws pertaining to water activities, and use good safety sense. Rangers will gladly answer questions.

Buckskin Point includes 67 campsites with water and electricity; 21 cabana units with electricity; sanitary dump station; shower and restroom facilities; boat launch area; children's playground; volleyball and basketball courts; Buckskin Market (groceries, beverages, tackle, swimwear); gas dock; Buckskin Visitor Center.

River Island Unit has 22 campsites with water; 13 tent sites without hookups; shower and restroom facilities; sanitary dump station; boat launch area; group use area with fire pit; shaded ramada for group use; River Island Market (groceries, tackle, fishing licenses, swimwear).

Contact the Buckskin Mtn. State Park, 54751 Highway 95, Parker, AZ 85344. ☎ (602) 667-3231; River Island Unit, ☎ (602) 667-3386.

Catalina State Park

Location: Northeast of Tucson, off Highway 89.

At the base of the Santa Catalina Mountains near Tucson, Catalina covers over 5,500 acres. A vast array of desert plants and wildlife inhabit the foothills, canyons, and streams of this high desert park. The landscape invites camping, picnicking, and birdwatching — more than 150 species of birds call the park home. An equestrian center provides a staging area for trail riders and plenty of trailer parking too. Miles of equestrian, birding, and hiking trails wind through the park and the Coronado National Forest.

Cattail Cove State Park

Location: 15 miles south of Lake Havasu City, off Highway 95.

Cattail Cove State Park provides the convenience of camping and the solitude of a campsite accessible only by boat. This popular spot and the nearby Sandpoint Resort and Marina offer visitors the comfort of home and the beauty of Lake Havasu.

Year-round water recreation has been raised to an art form her. Cattail Cove has modern lakeside camping facilities. It is an exceptional park. A unique feature here is that you can travel to over 140 boat-access-only campsites along the shore of Lake Havasu between Cattail Cove and Windsor Beach.

Write: PO Box 1990, Lake Havasu, AZ 86405, ☎ (520) 855-1223.

Dead Horse Ranch State Park

Location: In Cottonwood, off 10th Street.

Don't be alarmed by its name; this state park is next to the community of Cottonwood in the scenic Verde Valley and is alive with animal and human activity. Perhaps best known as a "nest" for birdwatchers, the park is also favored for picnicking, camping, canoeing, horseback riding, and stream and pond fishing. Walking trails meander along the shady banks of the Verde River. The park, with its full-facility campground, is also a good base for exploring other attractions in and around the Verde Valley.

Dead Horse Ranch State Park provides an opportunity to enjoy the scenic attractions of central Arizona. Camping, picnicking, fishing, hiking, and birdwatching are just a few of the pursuits open to park visitors. Over 100 bird species and 350 native plant species have been identified within the park. A major portion of the park's 325 acres borders the Verde River, allowing visitors to enjoy both desert and riparian vegetation and scenery.

Camping: 45 campsites (run on a first-come, first-served basis) with tables, grills, electricity, water, and a restroom area with showers. A sanitary dump station is near the entrance to the park.

Picnicking: Consisting of 26 sites, the shaded picnic area includes tables, grills, water, and restrooms. Trails begin at the picnic area and wind along the banks of the river. This is an excellent place to spot area wildlife, or to cool off in the water.

Fishing: The Verde River and the Park Lagoon provide great fishing opportunities. The four-acre lagoon is stocked with panfish, catfish, bass and, in winter months, trout. An Arizona fishing license is required at this and all state parks where fishing is permitted (see "Want to Know More..." section at the beginning of this chapter). Sorry, no swimming allowed in the lagoon.

Facilities available by reservation: A group campground accommodating up to 50 self-contained recreational vehicles. A group ramada for picnicking is available for groups of up to 50 people.

For further information, contact the Park Superintendent, Dead Horse Ranch State Park, PO Box 144, Cottonwood, AZ 86326. ☎ (602) 634-5283.

Fort Verde State Historical Park

Location: In Camp Verde, off Highway 260.

Fort Verde State Historic Park was a major base for General George Crook's scouts, soldiers and pack mules during the Indian campaigns of the 1870's. The scouts and soldiers were charged with squelching Apache and Yavapai Indian uprisings in the late 1800's. The homes on "Officer's Row" reflect the lives of frontier military personnel. The officers' quarters are open to visitors and depict what life was like on the frontier. The fort itself is a museum, located in the old headquarters buildings. It displays artifacts that explain the history and methods of frontier soldiering.

Military occupation of the Verde Valley began in 1865 at the request of settlers who had established farms near the Verde River at West Clear Creek junction, five miles south of the present Camp Verde. There they built a crude dam and diverted water to irrigate crops which promised to bring high prices in supply-short Prescott (then Arizona's territorial capital) and its hungry mining camps in the nearby hills.

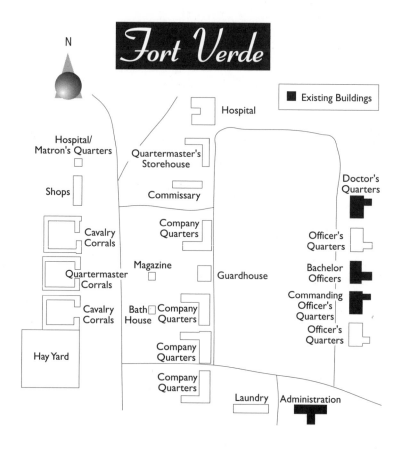

The influx of Anglo and Mexican miners severely disrupted the hunting and gathering methods of the Tonto Apache and Yavapai Indians. When Indians raided Verde Valley fields for corn, settlers called on the Army for protection. The late 1860's and early 1870's saw major conflicts.

The first military post (1865) overlooked the farms at West Clear Creek. The next post, Camp Lincoln, was a mile north of the present site and was used from 1866 to 1871. The current post was built in 1871-1873. It contained more than 20 buildings arranged around a parade ground. Like other posts of the period, it never had a wall around it and was never attacked. It served as a staging base for military operations in the surrounding countryside.

Two companies of cavalry and two of infantry were stationed at this post. The infantry built a wagon road west to Fort Whipple near Prescott and east to Fort Apache. Later called the Crook Road, after General George Crook, it speeded troops and supplies along the Mogollon Rim.

Between 1873 and 1875 nearly 1,500 Indians from various bands were placed on an 800-square-mile reservation with headquarters near the present town of Cottonwood. These Indians built an irrigation ditch and had 56 acres under cultivation in 1874. The entire population was, however, uprooted and moved to the San Carlow Agency near Globe. The 10-day trek in the cold of late February, 1875, resulted in death for some of the Indians from exposure, insufficient food, and a factional fight. Some of the people returned to the Verde Valley after 1900, but the former reservation had been opened to miners and settlers in 1877. After 1875, the Army's main concern was to keep Indians on the San Carlos and Fort Apache reservations. Renegades were hunted down by Indian scouts let by Al Sieber. An uprising in 1882 led to the last major battle with Apaches in Arizona. The insurgents were trailed to a canyon 37 miles east of Fort Verde. The ensuing Big Dry Wash fight resulted in the death or return to reservations of all renegades involved.

Camp Verde had been renamed Fort Verde in 1879 to signify permanence but, with the cessations of raids in 1882, the post became less important. It was abandoned in 1891 to the Department of the Interior, who sold it at public auction in 1899. Local citizens began a museum in the administration building in 1956, and donated several buildings to create Fort Verde State Historic Park in 1970. The site was placed on the National Register of Historic Places in 1971. The 10 acres include three officers' quarters, the foundations of two others, the administration building, and a portion of the parade ground.

For further information contact the Park Superintendent, Fort Verde State Historic Park, PO Box 397, Camp Verde, AZ 86322. ☎ (602) 567-3275.

Homolovi Ruins State Park

Location: 3 miles northeast of Winslow, Arizona. Take Interstate 40 to Exit 257; then go 1.3 miles north on Highway 87.

The Hopi elders tell of the migration of their ancestors, the Hisat'sinom, who moved from place to place to mark the boundaries of their homeland. Following the instructions of Masau, who in Hopi tradition owns this world and gave permission for humankind to live here, the people built their homes and planted their fields.

The ruined walls and scattered, broken pottery are eloquent testimony of the people that once lived in this place. The Homolovi pueblos, along with other prehistoric sites in northern Arizona, are still sacred to the Hopi people. Clan elders from the Hopi mesas up to 65 miles north of the park continue to make pilgrimages to these sites, renewing the ties of their people with the land.

There continue to be remarkable similarities between the architecture, pottery styles, and art motifs of the Hopi people and the prehistoric inhabitants of Homolovi.

Archeologists use the term Anasazi for the people who lived in this region during the 14th century. Every June and July, archeologists and volunteers carefully search the clay hills and windblown sands for new chapters in the story of these people and their forerunners, the Paleo-Indians and the Basketmakers. Much information has been lost through the years because of the destructive activities of misguided private collectors and the depredations of dealers in antiquities. Still, there are many remains that bear evidence of the ingenuity and skill of the Homolovi people.

Immediately to the north of Homolovi Ruins State Park live the Navajo people, the Diné. Although they arrived after the Homolovi left, the Navajo have also had great influence on the art and culture of northern Arizona.

Throughout the year, visitors to Homolovi Ruins State Park can explore the area and participate in a variety of programs provided by park staff members and volunteers. Please show respect for this sacred place. Although artifacts, ruins, and rock art within the park are protected by state and federal laws, each visitor should help presere this precious heritage by leaving things as they are found.

The park consists of over 4,000 acres at an elevation of 4,900 feet. More than 300 archeological sites have been identified within the park boundaries, including four major 14th-century pueblos.

The campground has 52 spaces, a restroom/shower building, picnic tables, and grills. A day-use area is available for picnics. Several hiking trails wind through pueblo ruins and petroglyphs; another leads to the historic Sunset Cemetery – all that remains of a settlement that developed from the Mormon immigration of 1876.

For further information, contact the Park Superintendent, Homolovi Ruins State Park, HC63 - Box 5, Winslow, AZ 86047. ☎ (602) 289-4106; TDD for the hearing impaired, ☎ (602) 289-4421.

Jerome State Historic Park

Location: In Jerome, off Highway 89-A.

Jerome's modern history began in 1876 when three prospectors staked claims on rich copper deposits. They sold out to a group that went on to form the United Verde Copper Company in 1883. The resultant mining camp of board and canvas shacks was named in honor of Eugene Jerome, the venture's principal backer. Hopes for the enterprise ran high, but the operating costs, especially for transportation, outstripped profits, and the company folded in less than two years.

It took the vision and vast financial resources of a new owner, William A. Clar, to bring in a narrow gauge railroad and reduce freighting costs. By the early 20th century, the United Verde was the largest producing copper mine in the Arizona Territory. Jerome was becoming a frame and brick town, and could boast of two churches, an opera house, a school, and several civic buildings.

In 1912, James S. Douglas purchased and began development of the Little Daisy Mine. By 1916, Jerome had two bonanza mines. Copper production peaked in 1929, but the depression and low grade ore deposits reversed the fortunes of the town.

The Little Daisy shut down in 1938. Phelps-Dodge took over the United Verde in 1935, but loss of profits brought the operation and Jerome's mining days to an end in 1953.

The Family

Grandfather Douglas began this family's involvement in copper mining up in Canada. Grandson Jimmy took to mining with gusto. It was in Nacozari, Mexico, that he acquired his nickname, Rawhide Jimmy, inspired by his use of rawhide to reduce roller wear on a cable car incline.

During development of the Little Daisy Mine in Jerome, his men cut into an extremely rich ore vein just in time for the soaring prices of World War I.

His eldest son, Lewis, chose politics instead of mining. In 1922, Lewis left Jerome for Phoenix where he served in the Sixth Arizona Legislature. His long career took him to Washington, D.C., and finally to England in 1947, as Ambassador to the Court of St. James.

James, the younger son, carried on the family tradition. His worldwide career in geology brought him home for work on the Little Daisy in its last years.

The Mansion

The Douglas mansion has been an eye-catching landmark in Jerome since 1916, when Rawhide Jimmy built it on the hill just above his Little Daisy Mine.

Jimmy designed the house as a hotel for mining officials and investors as well as for his own family. It featured a wine cellar, billiard room, marble shower, steam heat and, much ahead of its time, a central vacuum system. Douglas was most proud of the fact that the house was constructed of adobe bricks that were made on the site.

He also built the Little Daisy Hotel near the mine as a dormitory for the miners. Its concrete shell still stands.

Activities & Facilties

This former home is now a museum devoted to the history of the Jerome area and the Douglas family. It features exhibits of photographs, artifacts, and minerals in addition to a video presentation and a 3-D model of the town with its underground mines. One room, the Douglas library, is restored in period. The park is available for special functions and has been the site of many dances, weddings, meetings and luncheons. There are more displays outside along with a picnic area offering a beautiful panoramic view of the Verde Valley.

For further information, contact the Park Superintendent, Jerome State Historic Park, Box D, Jerome, AZ 86331. ☎ (602) 542-5381.

Lake Havasu State Park

Location: East of Winslow, off I-40.

Lake Havasu State Park has, in addition to breathtaking sunsets, two developed park units providing a wealth of recreational opportunities. Beaches, boating and camping are offered, not to mention the historic London Bridge, which connects the mainland to Pittsburg Point.

There are two distinct units at this water lovers' paradise. **Windsor Beach** is a wonderfully developed area in Lake Havasu City just north of the famed London Bridge. (London Bridge was dismantled at its original site in England and rebuilt in Arizona by developer Robert McCulloch in 1971.) Windsor Beach is popular for day use, camping (a new group campground is available by reservation), and launching all varieties of water craft.

Contact Arizona State Parks, 1300 W Washington, # 104, Phoenix, AZ 85007. ☎ (520) 855-2784.

Lost Dutchman State Park

Location: 5 miles northeast of Apache Junction off State Route 88.

Lost Dutchman State Park is rich with stories of lost gold and tall tales of the Old West. Situated at the base of the Superstition Mountains, it offers camping, picnicking and hiking. Access to nearby Tonto National Forest Land is also available.

Since the legendary Lost Dutchman Mine has never been redis-covered, the Superstition Mountains draw adventurers seeking lost gold as well as recreational riches. The park is an ideal starting point, fall through spring, for exploration of the Superstition Wil-derness. One of the Phoenix metro area's most popular desert lakes, Canyon Lake, is only 30 minute's drive from this camp-ground. Most visitors camp, picnic, or hike desert trails.

The sheer-walled escarpment of the Superstition Mountains looms above this 300-acre desert park set on the famous Apache Trail Highway. Ocotillo, palo verde, cholla, saguaro, and other plants of the Sonoran Desert thrive in this unspoiled setting steeped in beauty, history, and legend.

The Superstition Mountains (their name inspired by Pima Indian legends) are famous as the supposed site of the fabled Lost Dutch-man Mine. The story has many variations laced with tales of gold-thirsty Spaniards, Apache raiders, and of partnerships dis-solved by murder. Even today, zealous believers clatter through quiet canyons seeking the gold of Jacob Waltz.

The proximity of the Superstition Wilderness Area makes the park an ideal base for hikers and horseback riders. The park offers nature trails, 35 undeveloped campsites, restrooms, and picnic facilities, including tables, two group ramadas, and 13 single ramadas. Picnic supplies are available nearby and in Apache Junc-tion.

Enjoy the park for a family picnic, or as a halfway stop on the way to Canyon, Apache, and Roosevelt lakes.

For further information, contact the Park Superintendent, Lost Dutchman State Park, 6109 N. Apache Trail, Apache Junction, AZ 85219. ☎ (602) 982-4485.

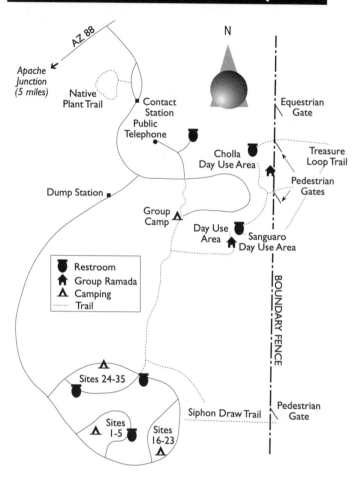

Lost Dutchman State Park

AZ 88

N

Apache
Junction
(5 miles)

Native
Plant Trail

Contact
Station

Public
Telephone

Equestrian
Gate

Cholla
Day Use Area

Treasure
Loop Trail

Pedestrian
Gates

Dump Station

Group
Camp

Day Use
Area

Sanguaro
Day Use Area

🛉 Restroom
🏠 Group Ramada
🔺 Camping
····· Trail

BOUNDARY FENCE

Sites 24-35

Sites
1-5

Sites
16-23

Siphon Draw Trail

Pedestrian
Gate

Lyman Lake State Park

Location: 1 mile off US Route 191 about 11 miles south of St. James.

Lyman Lake State Park is the place for camping, picnicking, fishing and waterskiing. A slalom water-ski course, hiking trails and ranger-guided petroglyph trail are offered. A large group-use area and concession area round out the amenities at this high-country (6,000 feet elevation) lake.

The welcoming committee at Lyman Lake is comprised of a small herd of buffalo, owned by the St. Johns Chamber of Commerce, that grazes beside the access road.

This 1180-acre park encompasses the shoreline of a 1,500-acre reservoir at an elevation of 6,000 feet. The lake was created in 1915 by damming the Little Colorado River. It is fed by snowmelt from the slopes of Mount Baldy and Escudilla Mountain, the second and third highest mountains in Arizona. Water is channeled into this river valley from a 790-square-mile watershed which extends into New Mexico.

Because of its size, Lyman Lake is one of the few bodies of water in northeastern Arizona with no size restrictions on boats. The west end of the lake is buoyed off and restricted as a no-wake fishing area (5 mph), where anglers fish for channel catfish, walleye, crappie, northern pike, and largemouth bass. The large remainder of the lake is open for all other types of water sports. Other park features include a swimming beach, picnic ramadas, boat rentals as well as hiking and rockhounding trails.

There are 38 hookup sites with cabana-type shelters, 21 developed campsites, a reservable group camping area with an all-weather building, a large day-use/picnic area with shade ramadas and a reservable group-use ramada. Also available are paved boat ramps, dump station, restrooms, showers, horseshoe pits, and a volleyball court. There are several pleasant, short hiking trails. A few primitive campsites located across the lake are accessible only by boat.

Lyman Lake really comes into its own during the spring, summer and fall. Summer days, with the highs in the 80s to low 90s, are perfect for fishing, swimming, leisure boating, waterskiing, rockhounding, hiking, or just plain relaxing.

Environmental education is now offered at Lyman Lake. The park is an island in time, taking you back to the early history of the native Americans. Staff offer tours of Indian petroglyphs dating from 10,000 B.C. to A.D. 1598. Personal experience in digging and restoration of an early Anasazi pueblo is another of the park's activities. The program includes a study of man's relationship to past and present ecosystems.

Regional points of interest include the Petrified Forest National Park, just 55 miles to the north; the White Mountains, 25 miles south.

For further information contact the Park Superintendent, Lyman Lake State Park, PO Box 1428, St. Johns, AZ 85936. ☎ (602) 337-4441.

McFarland State Historic Park

Location: In Florence, off Main Street.

Even though Florence is just one hour southeast of Phoenix, it has the look and feel of small town Arizona.

McFarland State Historic Park stood as the Pinal County Court-house from 1878-91. The original adobe structure houses the collections of Ernest W. McFarland, who began his career in law and politics in Pinal County and then went on to hold the highest office in each branch of Arizona Government. McFarland, creator of the Arizona State Parks Board, was a US Senator, Arizona Governor and State Supreme Court Justice.

Made from adobe bricks (mud and straw dried in the sun), the old courthouse is now a museum. The local doctor, dentist and sheriff all shared the building and inside you'll find the tools of their trades. The hospital room is authentic enough to keep you healthy after having seen the primitive instruments. Exhibits also feature artifacts from the history of the courthouse and Florence.

Special traveling exhibits display a variety of antiques, quilts and paintings. Our pride and joy, however is "Arizona's Attic! A Most Curious Collection." If you've ever wanted to see the door handle off Wyatt Earp's outhouse or the hairball of a cow, plan your visit now. This entertaining and educational exhibit will not encourage the pondering of great thoughts, but it will put a smile on your face.

McFarland State Historic Park is closed on Tuesdays and Wednesdays. ☎ (520) 868-5216.

Patagonia Lake State Park

Location: On SR 82 between Patagonia and Nogales.

Patagonia Lake State Park is set in the picturesque Sonoita Valley. It was created by the damming of Sonoita Creek in 1968. At 3,750-foot, the park has moderate temperatures throughout most of the year.

At 2½ miles long and 250 surface acres, Patagonia Lake is popular for a variety of recreational activities, including waterskiing, fishing, camping, picnicking and hiking. The lake is filled with bass, crappie, bluegill and catfish, and is stocked with rainbow trout during the winter. For anglers' sake, half the lake is designated a no-wake area. A level fishing pad is provided for wheelchair access. Because the lake attracts a multitude of water lovers during the summer months, waterskiing and jet skiing are prohibited on

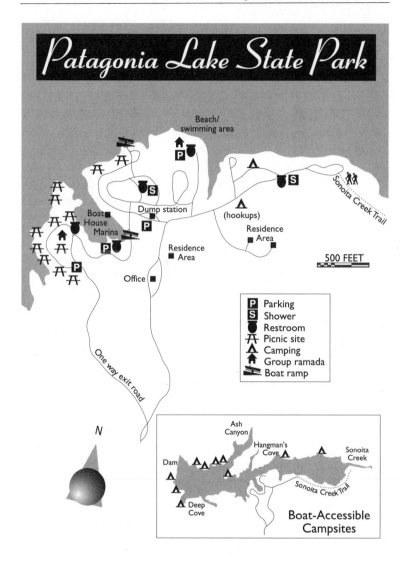

weekends from May through September. Camping ranges from undeveloped spots to sites with water and electric hookups.

There is also a half-mile hiking trail to Sonoita Creek, a concession-operated marina, restrooms, showers, picnic ramadas, and a swimming beach. Camping facilities include 95 developed sites, 10 hookup sites, and 12 lake (boat-access only) campsites. They are all available on a first-come, first-served basis. Group picnic areas may be reserved ahead of time.

For further information, contact the Park Superintendent, Patagonia Lake State Park, PO Box 274, Patagonia, AZ 85624. ☎ (602) 287-6965.

Picacho Peak State Park

Location: About 35 miles northwest of Tucson off Interstate 10.

Picacho Peak State Park, encompassing the sheer-sided peak that rises abruptly 1,500 feet from the desert floor, has camping, picnicking and hiking. This was the site for one of the few Civil War battles in the Southwest. The area is also noted for its spring wildflowers and desert nature study.

The prominent landmark here, Picacho Peak, rises majestically to a height of 1,500 feet above the desert floor, and is a magnet to skilled hikers. The less adventurous stroll along a trail at its base and marvel at the vibrant spectacle of blooming flowers.

Call ☎ (520) 466-3183 to speak directly with the park. Written information may be obtained from the Arizona Dept. of Parks and Recreation (see above).

Red Rock State Park

Location: Center for Environmental Education – Southwest of Sedona, off Highway 89-A and Lower Red Rock Loop Road.

Red Rock State Park Center for Environmental Education in Sedona offers visitors spectacular views, trails, and picnicking. In addition, special programs focus on the wildlife, natural and riparian systems of the park, which has Oak Creek running through it. School groups often use the park as an outdoor classroom, participating in environmental education activities.

Oak Creek curves through this 286-acre park, creating a diverse riparia habitat which abounds with plants and wildlife. Surrounded by Oak Creek Canyon's fiery red cliffs and cool green meadows, the park offers overnight facilities for accredited educational groups and day-use sites for hikers and picnickers. Camping is not allowed here. The park provides nature lovers with a fresh perspective on one of Arizona's most scenic areas.

The property was acquired by the Arizona State Parks Board in 1986. The 286 acres were originally part of the Smoke Trail Ranch, owned by Jack and Helen Frye. Jack Frye, then president of TWA Airlines, purchased the land in 1941 to develop into their vacation retreat and, in 1946, started building the House of Apache Fire, which still overlooks the land. The ranch consists of five parcels homesteaded by farmers in the late 1870s. The only homestead building remaining is the Willow House, built in 1931.

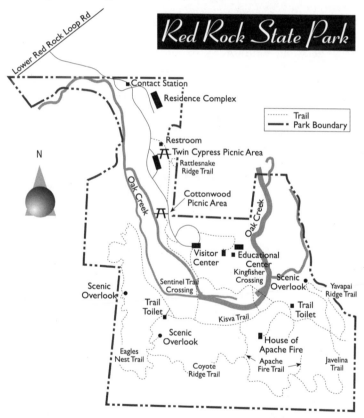

Red Rock State Park

Lower Red Rock Loop Rd

Contact Station

Residence Complex

Trail
Park Boundary

Restroom

N

Twin Cypress Picnic Area

Rattlesnake Ridge Trail

Oak Creek

Cottonwood Picnic Area

Oak Creek

Visitor Center

Educational Center

Kingfisher Crossing

Sentinel Trail Crossing

Scenic Overlook

Yavapai Ridge Trail

Scenic Overlook

Trail Toilet

Kisva Trail

Trail Toilet

Scenic Overlook

House of Apache Fire

Eagles Nest Trail

Coyote Ridge Trail

Apache Fire Trail

Javelina Trail

Environmental Education Programs

Providing Environmental education programs for children and adults is the primary objective. Programs for the general public are available on a regular basis, too. Specialized programs can be arranged by calling the park office. Theater, classroom, and limited overnight facilities for groups need to be reserved.

Help Protect Red Rock's Irreplaceable Resources!

- All visitors must remain on designated roads and trails to avoid damaging native vegetation.
- Pets are prohibited from entering the park.
- Charcoal fires are permitted in grills within the picnic areas. Wood gathering is prohibited.
- For protection of wildlife, swimming and wading are prohibited.
- Firearms, BB and pellet guns, bows, and fireworks are prohibited.
- Vegetation, wildlife, rocks, and artifacts may not be removed.
- Radios and other sound-producing devices must be kept on an individual hearing level to avoid disturbing wildlife and other visitors.
- All disposable items that are brought onto the park property must be taken out when you leave.

For further information, contact the Park Superintendent, Red Rock State Park, HC -Box 886, Sedona, AZ 86336. ☎ (602) 282-6907.

Riordan State Historic Park

Location: In Flagstaff, off Riordan Ranch Road.

Riordan State Historic Park features two homes built in 1904 by brothers Timothy and Michael Riordan. Connected by a "rendezvous wing," the structures offer a glimpse into the lives of the brothers, who played major roles in lumber, cattle, railroads, banking and politics in early Flagstaff and northern Arizona.

The Mansion

Tim and Mike Riordan were prominent pioneer Flagstaff businessmen who developed a successful logging industry. After marrying Caroline and Elizabeth Metz, their two families lived together in a unique early 20th-century mansion constructed in duplex fashion.

Built in 1904, the mansion is an impressive reminder of gracious living in a small frontier logging town. The rustic exterior incorporates log-slab siding, volcanic stone arches, and hand-split wooden shingles. The expansive home has 40 rooms, over 13,000 square feet of living area, and servant's quarters.

Mansion Tours

The interior of the mansion is open for guided tours only. Your guide will lead you through a richly furnished home filled with original artifacts, hand-crafted furniture, and personal mementos of the Riordan families. The building is designed in the American Arts and Crafts style, and contains an exceptional collection of Craftsman furnishings.

The Visitor Center

The park's visitor center maintains an interesting exhibit area, informative slide program, and a children's "touch table." A leaflet is provided for a self-guided tour of the grounds surrounding the mansion, and several brochures tell of Flagstaff's cultural, natural, and historic attractions. There are picnic tables and the opportunity for visitors to arrange special events, meetings, or private functions at the park.

For further information on the The Riordan Mansion, contact Riordan State Historic Park, 1300 Riordan Ranch Street, Flagstaff, AZ 86001. ☎ (602) 779-4395.

Roper Lake State Park

Location: South of Safford, off Highway 180.

Located at the foot of Mount Graham, Roper Lake is a haven for fishing, camping, picnicking, hiking and swimming.

Roper Lake State Park surrounds a man-made lake loaded with bass, bluegill and catfish. A level fishing pad is provided for wheelchair access. Hot springs feed the lake and developed hot tubs are available for visitors (day-use only).

The nearby Dankworth Ponds Unit features crappie as a popular catch. The lake and ponds are off-limits to gas-powered boats. Contact: ☎ (520) 428-6760.

Slide Rock State Park

Location: 7 miles north of Sedona, off Highway 89A.

The park surrounds a man-made lake loaded with bass, bluegill and catfish. Hot springs similar to those found at Roper Lake have been developed for visitor use. Dankworth Pond, six miles to the south, offers visitors day-use only.

Located in what many consider to be Mother Nature's finest playground, Slide Rock State Park is nestled in lush Oak Creek Canyon. The park takes its name from a 30-foot-long water slide worn in the rocks of the creekbed. Fishing, hiking, picnicking and nature-watching take on new dimensions among the canyon's red rock walls and pine forests. A thriving apple orchard is a unique attraction. The state has expanded parking and other facilities used by the waves of visitors who refresh themselves at Slide Rock during summer months. Several Forest Service campgrounds are nearby.

Tombstone Courthouse State Historic Park

Location: In the town of Tombstone, off US Route 80.

This park features a stylish Victorian building, constructed in 1882 and housing some of the history of the "town too tough to die." Artifacts, antiques and exhibits tell a tale of the Old West and a picnic area gives visitors a chance to eat lunch in the shadow of this historic structure.

In the silver-mining town of Tombstone, before the Cochise County Courthouse was built, justice was often decided by shootouts in the streets. The Victorian-style courthouse, built in 1882 at a cost of $50,000, stood out among its commonplace neighbors – a multitude of saloons and the infamous Boot Hill Cemetery. With law-

and-order efforts directed by a series of colorful sheriffs, Tombstone's past is captured in the thousands of artifacts exhibited here.

The Town of Tombstone

Tombstone reached its pinnacle of riches and fame, then faded, all within the short span of eight years. The West's wildest mining town owes its beginning to Ed Schieffelin, who prospected the nearby hills in 1877. Friends warned him that all he would ever find would be his own tombstone. But instead of an Apache bullet, he found silver – ledges of it – and the rush was on.

Miners soon built a shanty town on the closest level space to the mines, then known as Goose Flats. Remembering the grim prophecy given to Schieffelin, with tongue in cheek, they changed the name to Tombstone.

The year 1881 was an eventful one for the mining camp. The population reached 10,000, rivaling both Tucson (County Seat) and Prescott (Territorial Capital). The Earp and Clanton feud culminated in the famous gunfight near the OK Corral. A disastrous fire burned out much of the infant town, but it was immediately rebuilt. Schieffelin Hall was erected to provide legitimate theater and a meeting hall for the Masonic Lodge.

More than $37 million worth of silver had been taken from the mines when water began to seep into the shafts. Pumps were installed, but the mines were soon flooded to the 600-foot level and could not be worked. By 1886, Tombstone's heyday was over.

Tombstone Courthouse

As Tombstone's population grew, so did its political power. In 1881, the Arizona Legislature established Cochise County. No longer would the nearest county office be a long two-day ride.

Built in 1882 at a cost of nearly $50,000, the Cochise County Courthouse was a stylish building as well as a comforting symbol of law and stability in those dangerous times. It housed the offices of the sheriff, recorder, treasurer and board of supervisors. The jail was at the rear, under the courtroom. A series of renowned people held office there. John Slaughter was a local cattleman who, as sheriff, virtually cleared the county of outlaws.

Tombstone remained the county seat until 1929 when outvoted by a growing Bisbee. The last county office left the courthouse in 1931.

Except for an ill-fated attempt to convert the courthouse into a hotel during the 1940s, the building stood vacant until 1955, when it was acquired by the Tombstone Restoration Commission. They began its rehabilitation and development as an historical museum, which has continued under the State Parks Board since 1959. Exhibits and thousands of artifacts tell of Tombstone's colorful yesterdays.

For further information, contact the Park Superintendent, Tombstone Courthouse State Historic Site, Box 216 Tombstone, AZ 85638. ☎ (602) 457-3311.

Tonto Natural Bridge State Park

Location: 13 miles northwest of Payson, off Highway 87.

Tonto Natural Bridge State Park is the site of what is believed to be the largest natural travertine bridge in the world, over 400 feet long and 183 feet above sparkling Pine Creek. The span is 183 feet high over a 400-foot long tunnel that measures 150 feet at its widest point. Flowing springs and fern-draped grottoes line the narrow canyon upstream and, in a large grassy meadow above the bridge, a restored turn-of-the-century hotel provides a peek at an earlier time. Hiking, picnicking, historic setting and gift shop await visitors to this hidden gem.

The park combines the beauty of a natural wonder with the treasure of a National Register historic lodge. The park totals 160 acres, and offers picnicking and hiking. The Goodfellow Group Use Area may be reserved for special events such as reunions, weddings, and company picnics.

History

The discovery of the small but beautiful valley between Pine and Payson was documented in 1877 by Dave Gowan, a prospector who stumbled across the bridge while being chased by Apaches. Gowan hid for two nights and three days in one of several caves that dot the inside of the bridge. On the third day, he left the cave to explore the tunnel and the green valley surrounding it. Gowan claimed squatter's rights. In 1898, he persuaded his nephew, David Gowan Goodfellow, to bring his family from Scotland and settle the land permanently. After a week of difficult travel from Flagstaff, the Goodfellows arrived at the edge of the mountain and lowered their possessions down the 500-foot slope by ropes and burros into the valley.

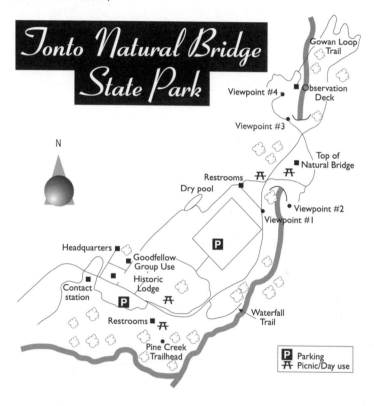

During the early 1900s, guest ranching grew into an Arizona industry. Between 1901 and 1908, David Goodfellow and his sons built a road and lodge at the site. The new facilities were promoted in newspapers and magazines, along with the benefits of Arizona's healthful climate and exotic scenery. As business rapidly grew, a new lodge was built in 1927. In 1987, the Clifford Wolfswinkel family gained ownership and renovated the lodge. It is filled with a variety of antiques and Gowan-Goodfellow family heirlooms. Ten bedrooms, six with adjoining porches, are named after colorful characters from Arizona's frontier days. The lodge is not yet available for overnight use, but plans are under way.

Kehl Spring Forest Service Campground is located several miles north on AZ 87 and Fire Road 300. This beautiful little campground is open May through November.

The geologic history of Tonto Natural Bridge extends back 1.7 billion years. The bridge was created somewhat like a building – from the foundation upward. It began with an ancient ridge of rhyolite that was submerged and covered with lava flows. The basalt was eroded and displaced, allowing Pine Creek to cut a narrow canyon. Precipitation seeped underground, created springs, and partially dissolved the limestone. The dissolved limestone in the spring water was redeposited as travertine at the mouth of the spring. Travertine forms the flat floor of the valley. Water from the creek began to get underneath a portion of the travertine, carving a "tube." Additional travertine was deposited on the top, eventually forming the natural bridge.

For further information contact the Park Superintendent, Tonto Natural Bridge State Park, PO Box 1245, Payson, AZ 85547. ☎ 602-476-4202.

Tubac Presidio State Historic Park

Location: 45 miles south of Tucson off Interstate 19 near Tubac.

Tubac Presidio State Historic Park highlights the contributions of Indians, Spaniards, Mexicans and Anglo Americans to the development of Arizona. Historic structures, exhibits and an underground view of the old Spanish fort that used to occupy the site take visitors back in time to learn about the history of Arizona's oldest European settlement.

History

Remnants of the military fort founded by the Spanish in 1752 have been uncovered by University of Arizona archeologists and preserved by Arizona State Parks. An underground display features portions of the original foundation, walls, and plaza floor of the Presidio (fort) de San Ignacio de Tubac. Spanish soldiers established the fort to control the local Pima and Apache Indians and serve as a base for further exploration of the Southwest. Also featured are a picnic area, an 1885 schoolhouse, and a visitor center with historic exhibits tracing Tubac's past from the days of Apache raids through its 1860 status as Arizona's largest frontier town.

The church and the military were the vanguards of Spanish frontier expansion throughout Mexico. The Jesuit, Eusebio Francisco Kino, established missions in Pimeria Alta (part of which is now southern Arizona) from 1687 to 1711 to convert and control Indians in the area. He established Tumacacori in 1691, and Tubac, then a small Pima village three miles to the north, became a mission farm or visita. Spaniards began to settle here during the 1730's and eventually controlled the land and the lives of the Indians.

In 1751, Luis Oacpicagigua, a Pima chief stirred by many grievances, led a revolt which drove the Spaniards southward. A military detachment was sent to the area, and peace was reestablished within three months.

Juan Bautista de Anza III, second commander of the presidio, organized two overland expeditions that resulted in the founding of San Francisco, in 1776 with 240 colonists from the provinces of Sinaloa, 63 of whom were from Tubac. Over 1,000 head of cattle, horses and mules were also gathered here for the expedition.

Apaches were a persistent threat to Tubac and the surrounding mines and ranches. When the military authorities moved the garrison from Tubac to Tucson in 1776, the unprotected settlers left their lands.

A company of Indian soldiers with Spanish officers was posted at Tubac in 1787. Apache reservations were established and the government provided supplies in an effort to keep the peace. But when Mexico won independence from Spain 1821, the new government lacked funds to continue supplying the Apaches, many of whom resumed a life of raiding. Apache raids and the lure of California gold resulted in Tubac's abandonment again. Forty-niners on their way to California described the village as having been recently deserted.

Tubac was included in the Gadsden Purchase of 1853, and was soon being resettled and developed by adventurers from the States as well as by former landowners. Charles D. Poston was instrumental in forming the Sonora Exploring and Mining Company, and served as the deputy clerk of southern Arizona. He performed marriages, granted divorces, baptized children, and printed his own money to pay company employees. The company had, in 1859, acquired a press which printed Arizona's first newspaper, *The Weekly Arizonian*.

Tubac's population steadily grew until, in 1860, it was the largest town in Arizona. The American Civil War, however, drained the region of troops, again leaving it unprotected from Apaches, and Tubac was soon deserted. Although the region was resettled after the war, silver strikes in the Tombstone area and the routing of the railroad through Tucson drew development interests away from Tubac, and the town never regained its earlier importance.

The excavation of the presidio in 1974 was then backfilled as a preservation measure. In 1976, a section was re-exposed in an archeological display enclosure where visitors can view portions of the original foundation, walls, and plaza floor of the 1752 structure. The display also takes a look into the culture of these people.

For further information contact the Park Superintendent, Tubac Presidio, Box 1296, Tubac, AZ 85646. ☎ (602) 398-2252.

Yuma Territorial Prison State Historic Park & Yuma Quartermaster Depot

Location: In Yuma, off I-8.

Yuma Territorial Prison State Historic Park features strap-iron and granite cell blocks, giving visitors a chance to see prison life in the early part of this century. Exhibits tell about the convicts, their crimes and punishments and how they spent their time while incarcerated.

Yuma Territorial Prison is living proof that there really was a wild West. More than 3,000 culprits, convicted of crimes ranging from polygamy to murder, lived in rock and adobe cells during the prison's 33-year life. Still standing are the cells, main gate, and guard tower. A fascinating museum details the prison's development and tells stories of the desperados, including 29 women, who did time there. Picnic tables and a ramada are provided.

The office of the Quartermaster Depot, one mile west of the prison, supplied Southwestern forts and soldiers from 1864 to 1883.

History

On July 1, 1876, the first seven inmates entered the prison at Yuma, and were locked into the new cells they had built themselves.

A majority served only portions of their sentences due to the ease with which paroles and pardons were obtained. Over 100 people died while serving their sentences, most from tuberculosis, which was common throughout the territory. Of the many prisoners who attempted escape, 26 were successful and eight died from gunshot wounds. No executions took place at the prison because capital punishment was administered by the county governments.

Despite an infamous reputation, evidence indicates that the prison was humanely administered, and was a model institution for its time. The only punishments were the dark cells for inmates who broke prison regulations, and the ball and chain for those who tried to escape. Prisoners had free time when they hand-crafted many items to be sold at public bazaars held at the prison on Sundays after church services. Prisoners also had regular medical attention, and access to a good hospital. Schooling was available for convicts, and many learned to read and write while serving time. The prison housed one of the first "public" libraries in the territory, and the fee charged to visitors for a tour of the institution was used to purchase books. One of the early electrical plants in the West furnished power for lights and ran a ventilation system in the cell block.

By 1907, the prison was severely overcrowded, and there was no room on Prison Hill for expansion. The convicts constructed a new facility in Florence, Arizona. The last prisoner left Yuma on September 15, 1909.

The Yuma Union High School occupied the buildings from 1910 to 1914. Empty cells provided free lodging for hobos riding the freights in the 1920s, and sheltered many homeless families during the Depression. Townspeople considered the complex a source for free building materials. This, plus fires, weathering, and railroad construction, destroyed the prison walls.

For further information contact the Superintendent, Yuma Territorial Prison, Box 10792, Yuma, AZ 85366-8792. ☎ (602) 783-4771.

National Parks

I have chosen to cover two of Arizona's national parks, both of which are well known and well worth a visit.

Grand Canyon

Location: From Flagstaff, take US 180 northwest for 81 miles
to reach the South Rim.

*S*omehow "Grand" does not tell how truly incomprehensible this canyon is. Words just can't begin to describe the Grand Canyon. Most people use such words as "marvelous," "stupendous," or "fantastic." Nothing compares. The scene continually changes as light plays off the rocks and clouds, creating shadows and contrasts. The world seems larger here with sunrises, sunsets, and storms taking on an added dimension to match the landscape. This is a land to humble the soul.

From many Grand Canyon viewpoints you can clearly see hiking trails winding down from the rim. Dangerously alluring, these footpaths rapidly descend from the cool shard forest at the rim to some of the most demanding hiking terrain.

Spanish explorers, led by Hopi guides, first came to the South Rim of the Grand Canyon in 1540. Over 200 years passed before another Spaniard, Father Escalante, became the first European to visit the Grand Canyon's northern rim.

The geography of the Grand Canyon region ensured that the North Rim would always be the "other" rim – the place where the Wild West held on. The Grand Canyon has always been more accessible from the south. Warms deserts to the east, west and south guarantee access to the South Rim during most of the year. On the North Rim, however, deep side canyons to the east and west challenge access. The only reasonable route to the park's North Rim is across the Kaibab Plateau, which rises to 9,000 feet and may receive up to 25 feet of snow in winter.

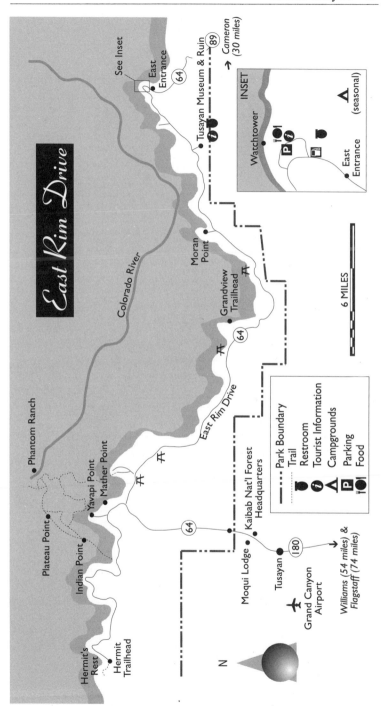

East Rim Drive

See Inset

East Entrance

64

→ Cameron (30 miles)

89

Tusayan Museum & Ruin

i

INSET

Watchtower

P *i*

East Entrance

▲ (seasonal)

Colorado River

Moran Point

Grandview Trailhead

64

6 MILES

East Rim Drive

Phantom Ranch

Yavapi Point

Mather Point

64

Plateau Point

Indian Point

Kaibab Nat'l Forest Headquarters

— · · — Park Boundary
· · · · · Trail
🚻 Restroom
i Tourist Information
▲ Campgrounds
P Parking
🍴 Food

Moqui Lodge

Tusayan

180

Grand Canyon Airport

Williams (54 miles) & Flagstaff (74 miles)

Hermit's Rest

Hermit Trailhead

N

Politics also played a role in the North Rim's isolation. North and west of the Grand Canyon lies a portion of land known as the Arizona Strip. Though it is related to Utah geographically, both Utah and Arizona claimed it. Had it not been for a determined writer, Sharlot Hall, "The Strip" (and with it, the North Rim) would likely have become part of the state of Utah.

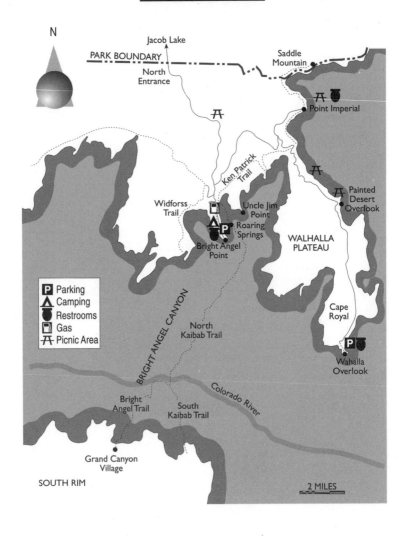

The Arizona Strip remained a noman's land well into the 20th century, though scattered Mormon settlements had succeeded in building large herds of cattle and sheep which grazed the green meadows of the North Rim. Sizeable deer herds attracted sportsmen.

But the North Rim is on the cusp of change. Numerous articles about this "undiscovered" part of the park and increasing population and mobility has resulted in the "re-discovery" of the North Rim. North Rim visitation has been growing by an average of five percent annually. At that rate increase, it will receive one million visitors by the year 2010.

Most visitors come to the South Rim (which is open all year). The North Rim (open mid-May through late October) has fewer facilities. It is over 200 miles one way by car from the South Rim to the North Rim, a five-hour drive at best.) The South Rim of the Grand Canyon averages 7,000 feet above sea level, the North Rim over 8,000 feet.

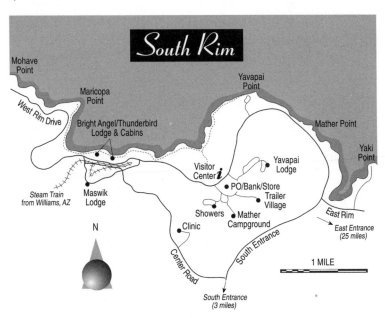

Summer temperatures on the South Rim are relatively pleasant (50-80° Fahrenheit), but inner canyon temperatures are extreme. Daytime highs at the river often exceed 100°. North Rim summer temperatures are cooler than those on the South Rim due to increased elevation.

Winter conditions at the South Rim can be extreme: expect snow, icy roads and trails, with possible road closures. Canyon views may be temporarily obscured during winter storms. Note that in such cases entrance fees are not refundable. Spring and Fall weather is unpredictable at best. Be prepared for sudden changes in the weather.

Hiking

The dayhiker, out for just a few hours, and the overnight backpacker must be equally prepared for the lack of water, extreme heat and cold, and isolation of the Grand Canyon. There are few places where the comforts of hotels, campgrounds, shops and restaurants are found so close to such a harsh environment.

Dayhiking, whether for one hour or from sunrise to sunset, can provide an excellent introduction to the inner canyon. During the extreme conditions of winter and summer, hiking without a heavy backpack is often more enjoyable than an overnight trip. As a dayhiker, you are entirely on your own. No permit is required and you do not need to inform rangers of your plans.

There are no loop trails for dayhikers; you will be hiking on the same trail in both directions. The scenery, however, is quite different, depending on which way you are facing. The dayhiker is as responsible as the backpacker for observing wilderness etiquette.

Overnight backpacking in the Grand Canyon provides a degree of solitude, wilderness and silence that is increasingly difficult to find.

All overnighters must obtain a permit. The main purpose of the permit is to control the number of people in one place at one time and thereby limit the impact from litter, human waste and trampling the ground. Permit requests should be mailed to:

Backcountry Office
PO Box 129
Grand Canyon, AZ 86023

Camping

Camping in the park on the South Rim is generally restricted to established campgrounds, although a few remote sites are available with a Backcountry Permit.

Mather Campground offers tent and RV camping (no hookups) in Grand Canyon Village. Reservations are strongly recommended and available by calling (800) 365-2267. Reservations may be made up to, but not more than eight weeks in advance. The campground is handled on a first-come, first-served basis from December 1 to March 1 of each year. Cost: $10 per site.

Trailer Village (adjacent to Mather Campground) offers RV sites with hookups; reservations may be made by calling ☎ (520) 638-2401. Cost $16 per site.

Desert View Campground (26 miles east of Grand Canyon Village, no hookups) is open mid-May through mid-October and operates on a first-come, first-served basis. Cost: $10 per site.

Ranger-Led Programs

National Park Service (NPS) rangers offer a wide variety of interpretive programs throughout the year on the South Rim, including a nightly evening program (indoors in colder weather, outdoors in the summer), and throughout the season the North Rim.

Bicycling

Bicycles are not available for rent at the park. If you plan to bring one, remember that you are subject to the same traffic rules as cars. Use extreme caution when riding on park roads; shoulders are narrow and vehicle traffic is heavy. The West Rim Drive is open through the year. Bicycles are not allowed on any park trails.

The North Rim of the Grand Canyon and the surrounding Kaibab National Forest offer opportunities for riding mountain bicycles.

Fishing

Fishing in the park requires an Arizona State fishing license. Licenses are available at Babbitt's general store in Grand Canyon Village on the South Rim and at Marble Canyon Lodge. Details on fishing regulations are available at the Backcountry Office.

Pets

Pets are allowed in the park but must be on a leash at all times. They are not allowed below the rim, nor are they allowed in park lodging or on park buses.

Fees

Entrance to the park is $10 per private vehicle, $4 for pedestrians or cyclists. Admission is for seven days and includes both rims. There are no refunds due to inclement weather.

For further information contact the Superintendent, PO Box 129, Grand Canyon, AZ 86023. ☎ (520) 282-3034.

Petrified Forest National Park

Location: Petrified Forest can be reached from either US 180 or I-40.

Eastbound: enter the park at the south entrance via US 180 from Holbrook, then travel north through the park, exiting eastbound on I-40.
Westbound: use the north entrance off I-40, proceed south through the park to US 180 to Holbrook and I-40.

The two-lane Park Road is 28 miles long. It winds along the rim of the Painted Desert, passes through archeological areas, and leads to many petrified wood sites. Several hours should be allowed to view the park. Due to narrow roads and periods of heavy traffic, bicycling is not recommended.

A land of contrasts, Petrified Forest National Park takes visitors to the beginning of dinosaurs, pre-historic peoples and modern wildlife. It is unmatched by anything else in the world.

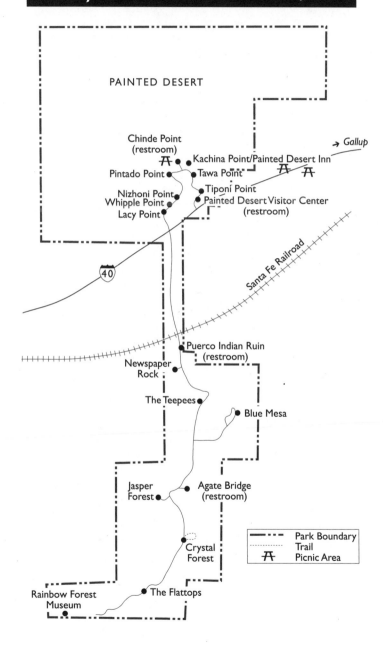

Petrified Forest National Park

PAINTED DESERT

→ Gallup

Chinde Point
(restroom)
Kachina Point/Painted Desert Inn
Pintado Point
Tawa Point
Tiponi Point
Nizhoni Point
Whipple Point
Painted Desert Visitor Center
Lacy Point
(restroom)

Santa Fe Railroad

40

Puerco Indian Ruin
(restroom)
Newspaper
Rock
The Teepees
Blue Mesa

Jasper
Forest
Agate Bridge
(restroom)

Crystal
Forest

Park Boundary
Trail
Picnic Area

Rainbow Forest
Museum
The Flattops

This high dry tableland was once a vast floodplain crossed by many streams. To the south, tall, stately pine-like trees grew along the headwaters. Crocodile-like reptiles, giant fish-eating amphibians, and small dinosaurs lived among a variety of ferns, cycads, and other plants and animals that are known only as fossils today. The tall trees fell and were washed by swollen streams into the floodplain. There they were covered by silt, mud, and volcanic ash, and this blanket of deposits cut off oxygen and slowed the logs' decay. Gradually, silica-bearing ground waters seeped through the logs and, bit by bit, encased the original wood tissues with silica deposits. Slowly the process continued, the silica crystallized into the quartz, and the logs were preserved as petrified wood.

That was about 225 million years ago. After that time, the area sank and was covered with freshwater sediments. Later it was lifted far above sea level and this uplift created stresses that cracked the giant logs. In recent times, wind and water have worked away the gradually accumulated lays of hardened sediments. Now the petrified logs and fossilized animal and plant remains are exposed and the Painted Desert has its present sculpted form.

The influence of man is readily seen on the landscape. Sites throughout the park tell of human history in the area for more than 2,000 years. No one knows the entire story, but there are signs of a cultural transition from wandering families to settled agricultural villages and trading ties with neighboring villages. The story fades around 1444.

In the mid-1800's US Army mappers and surveyors came into this area and carried back stories of the remarkable "Painted Desert and its trees turned to stone." Next, farmers, ranchers, and sightseers made their ways into the area. After a period of using the wood for souvenirs and numerous commercial ventures, territorial residents recognized that the supply of petrified wood was not endless. In 1906, selected areas were set aside as Petrified Forest National Park.

Today, the park is a high desert with low-growing plants, small animals and soaring birds – a place where the ancient past meets the modern world.

Hiking

The backcountry of the Petrified Forest includes 50,260 acres of established wilderness in two units: Painted Desert and Rainbow Forest. Day hikes are the most popular way to explore the back-country. Many features can be reached in a one-day trip, most lying within a few miles of the park road. There are few developed trails in Petrified Forest so the hiking is cross-country style. Clear air, lack of heavy vegetation, and a variety of landmarks combine to make conditions ideal for on-foot exploration.

The Painted Desert Wilderness offers 43,020 acres of colorful me-sas, buttes and badlands with scattered areas of grassland. Significant features include the Black Forest (petrified wood deposits), Chinde Mesa, and Pilot Rock.

The Rainbow Forest Wilderness has 7,240 aces of grassland and scattered badlands formations. There are several areas of petrified wood deposits within the wilderness.

There is no shade or water. Hikers should carry a good supply of liquids. A wide brimmed hat and long sleeved shirt will provide excellent sun protection. A gallon of water per person per day is recommended in summer months.

Painted Desert Rim Trail (1.2 miles round trip): An unpaved but easy trail winds along the Painted Desert rim between Taws and Kachina points. This is a land of contrasts. Stretching beyond the rim is the Painted Desert; brightly colored with banded hues of red, orange, pink and gray. Only a scant amount of vegetation grows among the deeply eroded soft clay hills.

Blue Mesa (1-mile loop): A steep paved trail leads from the top of the mesa down into the blue badlands – an amazing and beautiful area of banded, cone-shaped hills. Rainwater races down the hill-sides creating intricate patterns and miniature ravines. The blue-gray layers were deposited under a lake, while the pale red layers were deposited under a slow-moving river.

The Blue Mesa area is rich with plant and animal fossils. Look for fossils while hiking. Please do not disturb them.

Crystal Forest (0.8-mile loop): The trees of Crystal Forest once hid large amounts of beautiful smoky quartz, clear quartz, and purple amethyst crystal. Hike the paved loop trail and look for the smoky quartz crystals still found in a few logs along the trail. Admire the colorful "desert pavement" – a stony carpet of gravel, petrified wood chips and other rock fragments.

Long Logs (0.6-mile loop): This paved loop trail leads through the largest concentration of petrified wood in the park. The logs here lie criss-crossed on top of each other in log-jam formation. While at the northern end of the loop, look for some of the park's longest intact logs. The exposed portion of one directly adjacent to the trail measures 116 feet.

Agate House (0.9 mile round trip): This paved trail leads through petrified wood deposits and ends at the reconstructed Anasazi Indian pueblo. The eight-room pueblo sits on a knoll, 50 feet above the surrounding area. The walls of this unique ruin are built entirely of colorful petrified wood sealed with adobe.

Giant Logs (0.4-mile loop): Follow this paved loop past some of the park's most massive petrified logs. The largest log, known as "Old Faithful," measures 9'9" at the base.

Puerco Indian Ruins and Petroglyphs (0.5-mile loop): This short paved trail starts at the parking lot and takes you to a 76-room pueblo built by the Anasazi. Sections of their pueblo and a kiva (a religious ceremonial room) have been partially excavated.

Camping

There are no developed overnight accommodations in the park. Campgrounds and other facilities for overnight stays are available in neighboring communities. For those who wish to explore the park by extended hiking, backpack camping is permitted within the two wilderness units. Desert hiking requires the extra precautions mentioned above. Because of the slow rates of decomposition and growth in the desert and the fragile nature of the desert environment, minimum impact camping is very important.

Group size is limited to fifteen persons. By leaving no trace of your visit you can insure protection of wilderness values for all hikers and campers in the future. Fires are not allowed, but you may use a fuel stove for cooking. Overnight campers are required to have a wilderness permit.

Note: Petrified Forest National Park was established to preserve the area for future generations. Therefore, collecting petrified wood, plants, animals, fossils, artifacts or any other object in the park is strictly prohibited.

You may purchase petrified wood from commercial shops in or near the park. The wood sold in these stores is collected from private land outside of the national park.

For additional information contact the Superintendent, Petrified Forest National Park, Box 2217, Petrified Forest National Park, AZ 86028. ☎ (602) 524-6228.

Utah

State Parks

Utah is an eclectic mix of geological forms, flora, fauna and people. It is a natural vacationland with its massive mountains, vast forests, crystal-clear lakes, geological wonders, and its delightful summer climate. Whatever the time of year, whatever your favorite outdoor activity, you will find the parks of Utah to your liking. You can camp, boat, swim, fish, picnic, ride horseback, hike, enjoy nature trails, play golf, ride off-highway vehicles, or just relax with the ever-increasing number of cross-country skiers, snowmobilers, ice fishers, and hardy campers that make their way here.

In 1957, the Utah Legislature created what is today the Utah Division of Parks and Recreation. Lawmakers instructed the division to develop areas and to preserve and protect historical sites and scenic treasures.

The Utah State Park System began with only four parks: the old Utah State Prison site (which was later taken out of the park system); Territorial Statehouse; the Place Monument; and Camp

Floyd. A $20,000 grant from the Rockefeller-Jackson Hole Preservation Foundation provided initial funds.

For more than 30 years, the division has been expanding the park system. It now has over 35 developed and six undeveloped parks in Utah – that adds up to 95,000 acres of land and more than a million surface acres of water beckoning visitors!

Services

Standard boating facilities include concrete launching ramps, loading docks, and parking for vehicles and boat trailers. Camping, picnic sites, and restrooms are also available. The very least a park has to offer will include launching ramps, loading docks, trash containers, and portable or vault restrooms.

The following state parks provide mooring and/or dry storage for boats and recreation equipment: Antelope Island, Bear Lake, Deer Creek, East Canyon, Great Salt Lake, Minersville, Otter Creek, Rockport, Utah Lake, and Willard Bay.

Fishing and boating services, such as gasoline and oil, groceries, sundries, fishing tackle, refreshment stands, and rental boats are available on site or nearby the following parks: Antelope Island, Bear Lake, Deer Creek, East Canyon, Great Salt Lake, Otter Creek, Rockport, Scofield, Starvation, and Utah Lake.

Bicycling

In the past several years, biking opportunities in Utah have expanded dramatically. New trails and maps have opened wild and remote areas formerly inaccessible to cyclists. Several ski resorts now offer summer chairlift mountain biking. Multi-day routes link distant regions, trail hubs and a dazzling display of terrain. For more information, ☎ (800) 200-1160 for the *Bicycle Utah Guide.*

River Running

Utah is renowned world-wide for its whitewater rafting. Coursing through southeast Utah are the mighty Colorado and Green rivers, as well as the historic San Juan River. With no dam to control its flow of water, the Colorado through Cataract Canyon offers some of the largest rapids in North America. The Green River is an ideal trip for families. The San Juan is noted for its exceptional archeological and geological excursions. The state's 41 professional river outfitters offer a wide variety of tours and services. Ask around and compare prices and services.

Fishing

Utah has over 1,000 fishable lakes and numerous fishing streams. Species range from the popular rainbow and cutthroat to large mackinaw and brown trout to striped bass, walleye, bluegill, whitefish, the Bonneville cisco and many others. Fishing is open year-round in Utah.

Hunting

Deer, elk, antelope, pheasant, duck, geese, sage grouse, forest grouse, chukar partridge, mourning dove, wild turkey, cottontail rabbit and snowshoe rabbit are commonly hunted in Utah. Special game permits are decided by a drawing. Applications for these are taken only between May 5 to 25. The application period to hunt bear, mountain lion and bobcat is mid-October to mid-November. Most species of wildlife are protected in Utah. Hunting is allowed in most public areas of the state, except the national parks and monuments, as well as some state parks. Check with the Utah Division of Wildlife for regulations.

Boating

Boats with motors are not permitted on Palisade Reservoir (Manti) or on the Jordan River.

Boating Rules & Laws

The Utah Division of Parks and Recreation administers Utah's boating laws. Laws and suggested safety equipment are explained in the booklets *Highlights from Utah Boating Laws and Rules* and *Utah*

Boating Laws and Rules. These are available by calling ☎ (801) 538-7221. Many boaters are increasing their nautical skills and knowledge by taking advantage of the popular boating education home study course, *Utah Boating Basics.* Copies of the course book are available at all state parks, regional offices, and the administrative office in Salt Lake City (see the Want To Know More? section of this chapter for addresses).

Off the Highway

Because so much of Utah is public land, great off-highway riding areas are never far away. Care must be taken to insure a safe, enjoyable experience while protecting the environment. The Utah Division of Parks and Recreation, National Forest Service, and Bureau of Land Management work together in providing thousands of miles of trails for riding enjoyment. Detailed information is available by contacting one of these agencies. Addresses are listed in the Want to Know More? section, below.

All-Terrain Vehicles & Off-Highway Motorcycles

Utah has a number of excellent all-terrain vehicle and off-highway motorcycle riding areas within, adjacent to, or originating from state parks. The following parks offer on-site or nearby riding opportunities.

Coral Pink Sand Dunes	Otter Creek
Dead Horse Point	Palisade
Escalante	Plute
Fremont Indian	Quail Creek
Goblin Valley	Scofield
Green River	Starvation
Huntington	Steinaker
Kodachrome Basin	Wasatch Mountain
Millsite	Yuba

Off-Highway Vehicle Laws

The Utah Division of Parks and Recreation, in cooperation with other state, federal, and private land management agencies, administers Utah off-highway vehicles (OHV) laws.

- Registered OHVs may be operated on public lands, streets, or highways that are signed or designated as open to OHV use.
- Most inner-park roads are public highways. State law requires that motorized vehicles and operators using public highways be licensed. The US Forest Service, Bureau of Land Management, and Utah Division of Parks and Recreation have travel maps indicating public lands where OHV use is permitted.
- Persons 17 years of age and under must wear protective headgear while operating an OHV on public lands or roads. It is recommended that all riders, no matter what their age, wear helmets.
- No one under eight years of age may operate an OHV on public lands. Drivers eight through 15 years of age must possess an OHV education certificate issued by the division. Drivers sixteen years of age and older must possess a valid driver's license or an OHV education certificate.

Laws and suggested safety equipment are explained in the booklets Highlights from *Utah's Off-Highway Vehicle Laws and Rules*. Copies are available at all state parks, regional offices, and the administrative office in Salt Lake City.

OHV Education Program

Education certificates will be issued to anyone eight years of age and older who completes the Utah OHV education course. For information, contact the Utah Division of Parks and Recreation OHV Training Center at ☎ 800-OHV-RIDE.

Snowmobiling

Thousands of Utahns and out-of-state visitors snowmobile through mountain forests and rolling hills. The Utah Division of Parks and Recreation provides facilities and also enforces the laws. It grooms nearly 850 miles of prime snowmobile trails, removes snow from parking lots, and manages sanitary facilities throughout the state.

Snowmobile rentals, warming facilities, and food services are available at Wasatch Mountain State Park.

Principal Trailheads

Wasatch Mountain/American Fork Canyon. Originating from Wasatch Mountain State Park at Midway, interconnecting Park City, American Fork Canyon, Alpine Loop and Cascade Springs.

Mirror Lake Highway. Joining Kamas, Bear River Service, Soapstone, Woodland, Lake Creek, and Wolf Creek canyons.

Monte Cristo/Hardware Ranch in northern Utah. Interconnecting 90 miles of trails in Ogden Logan, and Blacksmith Fork canyons.

Skyline Drive in central Utah. Providing trails from Scofield, Tucker Rest Area, Joe's Valley, Ephraim, Manti, Ferron, and Fairview canyons.

Brian Head, Navajo Lake, Duck Creek Village, Strawberry Point, and **Cedar Breaks** in southern Utah.

Fish Lake National Forest near Fish Lake.

Red Cloud Loop north of Vernal.

Maps are available at all state parks, regional offices, and the administrative office in Salt Lake City (see Want to Know More?).

Camping — Primitive to Plush

Utah state park visitors will find more than 1,200 campsites ranging from primitive to plush! The most basic campgrounds have pit or vault toilets and bare necessities for outdoor living. Standard campsites are equipped with barbecue grills, picnic tables, flush toilets, culinary water, parking pads, and sanitary disposal stations. Some offer hot showers and utility hookups.

Reservations

Reservations for group-use areas and individual campsites are available at all developed parks. Individual campsite reservations may be made from three to 120 days in advance. Group reservations may be made one year in advance.

To make a reservation, ☎ (801) 322-3770 or, toll-free, (800) 322-3770, from 8 am to 5 pm, Monday through Friday. Reservations are not required but are advised. Unreserved sites are available on a first-come, first-served basis.

User Fees

Day-use and camping fees are charged most state parks. Additional fees are charged for other services, such as ice skating, roller skating, golfing, boat mooring, chalet or visitor center rentals, and group-use facilities. Fees are subject to periodic change. Contact the park itself, or the regional office or the administrative office in Salt Lake City for current rates.

Facilities for the Physically Challenged

Many of Utah's state parks have fully-accessible facilities for the disabled. Development is ongoing. Contact the park directly.

Events for All Seasons

Utah state parks have special activities for everyone – runners, bikers, boaters, cross-country skiers, golfers, history buffs, off-highway vehicle enthusiasts, and nature lovers.

Watchable Wildlife

There are nearly 100 designated wildlife viewing sites in Utah, many of which are in state parks. Look for the binocular logo on road signs as you travel the state.

Want to Know More?

1596 West North Temple
Utah Div. of Wildlife Resources
Salt Lake City, UT 84116-3195
(801) 538-4700

Bureau of Land Management
324 South State Street, Suite 301
PO Box 45155
Salt Lake City, UT 84145-0155
(801) 539-4001

US Forest Service Regional Office
2501 Wall Avenue
Ogden, UT 84401-2394
(801) 625-5306

National Park Service
PO Box 25287
Denver, Colorado 80225-0287
(303) 969-2000

Utah Tourism & Recreation Information Center
Utah Travel Council
Council Hall, Capitol Hill
Salt Lake City, UT 84114-1369
(801) 538-1467

Utah Division of Parks & Recreation

Administrative Office
1636 West North Temple, Suite 116
Salt Lake City, UT 84116-3156
(801) 538-7220

Eastern Region Office
89 East Center Street
Moab, UT 84532-2330
(801) 259-8151

Northeast Region Office
PO Box 309
Heber City, UT 84032-0309
(801) 645-8036

Northwest Region Office
1084 North Redwood Road
Salt Lake City, UT 84116-1555
(801) 533-5127

Southwest Region Office
585 North Main Street
PO Box 1079
Cedar City, UT 84720-1079
(801) 586-4497

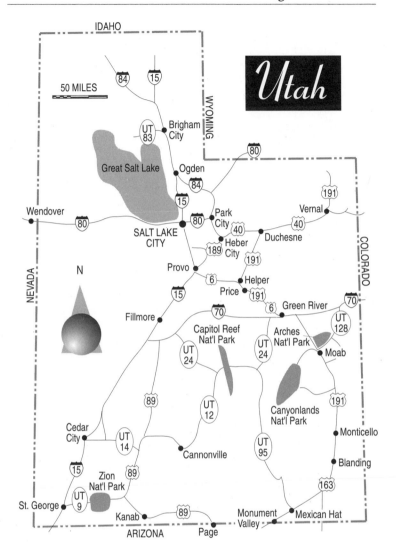

Anasazi Indian Village State Park

Location: Near the picturesque ranching town of Boulder on SR 12.

This ancient Indian village in the heart of Utah Canyon Country was one of the largest Anasazi communities west of the Colorado River. The site is believed to have been occupied from A.D. 1050 to

1200. Even though the village remains largely unexcavated, many artifacts have been uncovered and are on display in the museum.

Facilities in the park are few. Group and individual picnic areas are available. There is no camping.

For further information contact Anasazi Indian Village State Park, PO Box 1329, Boulder, UT 84716-1329. ☎ (801) 335-7308.

Antelope Island State Park

Location: Reached via a 7½-mile paved causeway. From I-15, take Syracuse Exit 335 west for seven miles.

Antelope Island State Park is the largest island in the Great Salt Lake. Activities on the island include saltwater bathing, sunbathing, camping, hiking, horseback riding, picnicking, photography, birdwatching and observing wildlife in a natural habitat. You also may enjoy spectacular sunsets and panoramic views of the Great Salt Lake.

Buffalo, antelope, mule deer, upland game birds and waterfowl are some of the animals you may see here. You might even catch sight of elk, badger, coyote, fox, golden eagle or bobcat.

Facilities at this park include modern restrooms, hot showers, picnic shelter, group-use pavilion, boat launching ramp and marina. Cyclists, equestrians and hikers may traverse more than 30 miles of roads and trails. A concessionaire provides food, drinks, gifts and guided tours to the southern end of the island.

For further information, contact Antelope Island State Park, 4528 West 1700 South, Syracuse, UT 84075-6861. ☎ (801) 773-2941.

Bear Lake State Park

Location: On US Highway 89, two miles north of Garden City.

Bear Lake is nestled high in the Rocky Mountains on the Utah-Idaho border. Waterskiing, swimming, and sailing are favorite activities. Fishing is for cutthroat, mackinaw, and whitefish. Bear

Lake is famous for its annual January cisco run. Three state-owned facilities provide boating, camping and picnicking. The marina has a sheltered harbor, an 80-foot-wide concrete launching ramp, 176 seasonal boat slips, sanitary disposal station, 15 shoreline campsites, modern restrooms, hot showers and a visitor center.

Bear Lake Rendezvous Beach is on the south shore of the lake near Laketown on State Route 30. It extends for 1¼ miles and offers 138 campsites, modern restrooms, hot showers, and utility hookups. A wide, sandy beach provides excellent camping, picnicking and small watercraft activity. Rendezvous Beach is a popular area for groups and family reunions. A local concessionaire has small boats for rent.

Bear Lake Eastside is 10 miles north of Laketown. Activities include scuba diving, boating and fishing. There is a primitive campground and a 28-foot-wide concrete boat launching ramp.

For further information, contact Bear Lake State Park, PO Box 184, Garden City UT 84028-0184. ☎ (801) 946-3343.

Camp Floyd/Stage Coach Inn State Park

Location: 25 miles southwest of Lehi on State Route 73.

*T*his former military post quartered the largest troop concentration in the United States from 1858 to 1861. About 400 buildings housed the 5,600 troops sent to suppress an assumed Mormon rebellion. The troops returned east in 1861 for Civil War duty. Only a cemetery remains as silent evidence of turbulent Camp Floyd.

Nearby Stagecoach Inn was an overnight stop on the historic overland stage and pony express route. A two-story adobe and frame hotel has been restored with original period furnishings. It is open daily from Easter weekend through October 15.

For further information, contact Camp Floyd/Stage Coach Inn State Park, PO Box 446, Riverton, UT 84065-0446. ☎ (801) 768-8932 (April -November).

Coral Pink Sand Dunes State Park

Location: 12 miles from US Highway 89, near Kanab.

Contrasted by blue skies and steep red cliffs and outcroppings, Coral Pink Sand Dunes State Park is the perfect setting for camping, off-road riding, picture taking, hiking or just relaxing and playing in the sand.

The park was established in 1963 with land purchased from the USDI Bureau of Land Management.

Geology

The dunes here are created by wind heading between Moquith and Moccasin mountains. The wind is funneled through this notch, gaining speed to a point where it can carry sand grains from the eroding Navajo sandstone. This phenomenon is known as the Venturi Affect. Once the wind passes through the gap and into the open valley, its speed decreases and the sand is deposited.

Hiking

The sand dunes at the park are a unique and interesting place to hike. You will discover many other hikes adjacent to the park, including the following:

Harris Mountains - North of the park. These "mountains" offer scenic views of the sand dunes and of Zion National Park.

Moquith Mountains - From the east boundary of the park. Vantage points at the top of the sand dune offer views of Kanab Canyon and the North Rim of the Grand Canyon.

South Fork Indian Canyon Pictographs - Ancient Indian paintings are at the bottom of South Fork Indian Canyon. The trailhead is approximately four miles northeast of the park and is accessible via hiking, OHV and four-wheel-drive vehicles.

Plants & Animals

At an elevation of 6,000 feet, Coral Pink Sand Dunes receives relatively high amounts of precipitation. This moisture allows for a wide variety of plants, including stands of ponderosa pine, dune grasses more than six feet tall and beautiful wildflowers that reach their peak in June.

Common mammals in the park include mule deer, coyotes, kit foxes, jack rabbits and many small rodents. The dunes also support a diverse population of insects, including the coral pink tiger beetle that is found only here. Melting snow often creates small ponds here that support amphibians such as salamanders and toads.

Off-Highway Vehicles

Coral Pink Sand Dunes includes 1,000 acres of play area for off-road vehicle enthusiasts. Hundreds of miles of trails and several developed four-wheel roads are on USDI Bureau of Land Management land adjacent to the park.

Off-highway vehicles are permitted on the dunes, but strict regulations apply. OHV riders should contact park personnel for laws and rules before venturing out.

Nearby Points Of Interest

The park is an excellent base camp for exploring Utah's extraordinary scenery. Within a short drive are Cedar Breaks National Monument, Kodachrome Basin State Park, Lake Powell, and Zion, Bryce Canyon and Grand Canyon national parks. Park personnel will gladly help plan an outing for you and your family.

Special Features

Park facilities include a 22-unit campground, modern restrooms, hot showers, sewage disposal station, a boardwalk overlook trail and a half-mile nature trail. Each roomy campsite has pull-through parking, picnic table and barbecue grill. A resident ranger and a small visitor center are also on site.

Five picnic sites, including a large group-use area, are adjacent to the dunes. Picnic sites are equipped with barbecue grills and picnic tables on concrete pads. The group site has a fire pit ideal for Dutch oven cooking.

For further information, contact Coral Pink Sand Dunes State Park, PO Box 95, Kanab, UT 84741-0095. ☎ (801) 874-2408.

Dead Horse Point State Park

Location: Dead Horse Point is on State Route 313, 18 miles off Highway 191 near Moab.

Dead Horse Point is perhaps Utah's most spectacular state park. Towering 2,000 feet directly above the Colorado River, the point provides a breathtaking panorama of Canyonlands' sculptured pinnacles and buttes.

The Story of Dead Horse Point

Before the turn of the century, mustang herds ran wild on the mesas near Dead Horse Point. The unique promontory provided a natural corral into which the horses were driven by cowboys. The only escape was through a narrow, 30-yard neck of land controlled by fencing. Mustangs were then roped and broken, with the better ones being kept for personal use or sold to eastern markets. Unwanted culls or "broomtails" were left behind to find their own way off the point.

According to one legend, a band of broomtails was left corralled on the point and the gate was supposedly left open so the wild horses could return to the open range. For some unknown reason, the mustangs never found their way out. They died of thirst within sight of the Colorado River, 2,000 feet below.

Plants & Animals

Vegetation and wildlife in this desert environment exist on a severely limited water supply. Plants have adapted by diminishing the size of their leaves, which means they lose less water through evaporation.

Dead Horse Point State Park

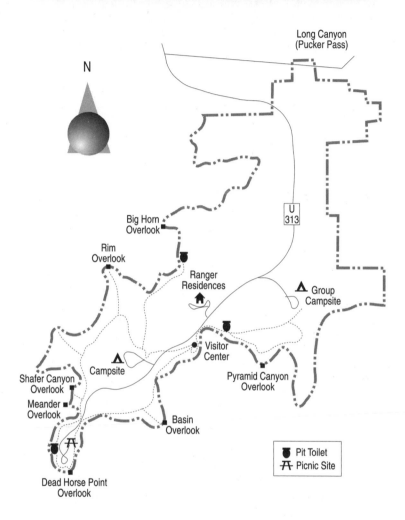

Most of the animals are nocturnal. They venture out in the evenings when the relentless heat has subsided and there is less need for water. Other wildlife and vegetation may have dormant periods depending upon precipitation patterns.

These desert wildlife has only a slight edge on the environment. Please do not disturb them in their struggle for existence.

Facilities

The visitor center offers exhibits, an orientation program and a self-guided nature trail. Short guided walks are provided during the high season. The center presents summer evening programs between mid-May and mid-September.

Kayenta Campground is the main campsite area with 21 camping units, modern restrooms, covered picnic tables, electrical hookups and sewage disposal stations. Available water is hauled from Moab. To help with water conservation, recreational vehicles should fill water tanks before coming to the park.

Geological Sketch

The overlook at Dead Horse Point is 6,000 feet above sea level. Two thousand feet below, the Colorado River winds its way from the Continental Divide in Colorado to the Gulf of California, a distance of 1,400 miles.

From the overlook, canyon erosion may be viewed on a grand scale. This process has taken approximately 150 million years. Much of it is caused by the river slicing down into the earth's crust as land is forced upward. These powerful forces are still sculpturing the fantastic shapes of these precipitous bluffs and towering spires.

General Information

Dead Horse Point is a promontory of stone surrounded by steep cliffs. Watch children and pets closely.

The park and developed campground are accessible year-round. All camping is limited to 14 days in any 30-day period.

Clear skies and little vegetation allow evenings to cool rapidly. Mornings warm equally as fast. Daily summer temperatures sometimes drop as low as 40°F at night and climb to over 90° the following day. Very few days exceed 100°.

The winter season is short with very little snow. Nights may be cold from December through February, but daytime temperatures are generally pleasant.

Spring and autumn days are long and, generally, agreeable. Annual precipitation is about 10 inches per year.

For further information, contact Dead Horse Point State Park, PO Box 609, Moab, UT 84532-0609. ☎ (801) 259-2614.

Deer Creek State Park

Location: 7 miles southwest of Heber.

Deer Creek Reservoir lies in the southwest corner of beautiful Heber Valley and consistently provides some of Utah's finest fishing. **Sailors take note:** Predictable canyon winds make sailing great.

Facilities in Deer Creek State Park include a concrete boat launching ramp, modern restrooms with showers, sewage disposal and fish cleaning stations, 32-unit campground, and paved parking area. Two concessionaires offer a restaurant, boat rentals, gasoline, and sundries.

For further information, contact Deer Creek State Park, PO Box 257, Midway, UT 84049-0257. ☎ (801) 654-0171.

East Canyon State Park

Location: Northeast of Salt Lake City on SR 65.

East Canyon Reservoir is a 680-acre boating and fishing paradise nestled in the mountains. Recreationists will find a wide concrete launching ramp, paved parking area, modern restrooms, showers, fish cleaning station, and a 31-unit campground with a large overflow area. Two spacious pavilions with electricity are available for groups. A concessionaire offers boat rentals and a refreshment stand.

For further information, contact East Canyon State Park, 5535 South Highway 66, Morgan, UT 84050-9694. ☎ (801) 829-6866.

Edge of The Cedars State Historic Monument

Location: Just northwest of Blanding at 660 West, 400 North.

Edge of the Cedars State Historical Monument is the site of an Anasazi Indian ruin and a modern museum facility. It was established as a state historical monument in 1974. In late 1978 the museum facility was completed and opened to the public. It is operated by the Utah State Division of Parks and Recreation.

The museum deals with the various cultures that have influenced the San Juan County area of southeastern Utah. These include the prehistoric Anasazi Indians, the Navajo Indians, the Ute Indians, and early Anglo settlers.

Facilities at the museum include restrooms, two exhibit halls, an auditorium, research and work rooms, offices and a contemporary Indian crafts demonstration area and shop.

Edge of The Cedars Ruin

The Edge of the Cedars Indian ruin is a small Anasazi village that was occupied roughly from 750 A.D. to 1220 A.D. The site consists of six distinct habitation and ceremonial complexes which lie in a general north-south alignment on top of the ridge in back of the museum and overlooking Westwater Canyon.

Complexes #1, #2, #3, and #5 are unit-type pueblos, while #4 is a large block of rooms with an associated Great Kiva. The sixth complex is a row of adjoining surface rooms at the southern end of the site.

The Edge of the Cedars Ruin was discovered by the first Anglo settlers in 1905. No development had taken place at the site, however, until the late 1960's. Approximately 25% of the site was excavated from 1969 to 1972 by Weber State College. Following the excavations, some stabilization was done by capping the excavated walls.

An ongoing excavation and/or stabilization program is planned for each season. Visitors are encouraged to walk among the ruins, but should not climb on the walls.

In 1970 the Edge of the Cedars ruin was placed on the Utah State Register of Historic Places and, in 1971, it was placed on the National Register of Historic Places.

Escalante State Park

Location: 44 miles east of Bryce Canyon National Park.

This park is a showcase of petrified wood. Backcountry explorers might see fossilized dinosaur bones or remnants from the ancient Fremont Indians who inhabited the area nearly 1,000 years ago. Add to this the visitor center, campground and Wide Hollow Reservoir, and you have a complete recreation experience.

Activities

Two established trails take you through vast deposits of the most beautiful petrified wood found anywhere. Some pieces are nearly five feet wide!

Wide Hollow Reservoir, located partially within park boundaries, offers great fishing for rainbow trout and bluegill. Many visitors like to swim in the cool water, while others enjoy lounging on sunny shores or watching the many species of bird and waterfowl.

Camp and picnic in a modern, 22-unit campground complete with tables, fire pits, barbecue grills, culinary water, restrooms with hot showers, and sanitary disposal station.

Area Attractions

The Escalante area is a veritable wonderland of scenic beauty. A base camp in the park puts you within a few miles of the high-mountain lakes and forests of Boulder Mountain, remote canyons of the Escalante River and slick rock desert country of the famous Hole-in-the-Rock crossing at Lake Powell.

Plants & Animals

The surrounding area is typical of the Upper Sonoran life zone. Trees are mostly pinyon and juniper, with stands of cottonwoods along the lake shore. Many species of wildflowers share the park with small rodents, lizards, waterfowl, birds, deer and coyotes. Escalante State Park is listed in the *Utah Wildlife Viewing Guide* as one of the few wetland bird viewing sites in southern Utah.

History

Escalante State Park was established in 1963 with land purchased from the US Bureau of Land Management. Additional land was bought in 1972 to include part of the shoreline of Wide Hollow Reservoir. The campground and ranger housing were completed in the spring of 1977; the visitor center in 1991; and the bridge and paved road in 1992.

Wide Hollow Reservoir was constructed in 1954. Its water is used by the town of Escalante for irrigation.

For further information, contact Edge of the Cedars State Park, PO Box 788, Blanding, UT 84511-0788. ☎ (801) 678-2238.

Fort Buenaventura State Park

I-15 southbound: Take Ogden Exit 344B to 31st Street Westbound and follow the signs.
I-15 northbound: Take Ogden Exit 346 and follow the signs.
Downtown Ogden: Go west on 24th Street across the viaduct. Take your first left on A Avenue.

One of the most fascinating periods in Western American folklore is the Mountain Men era. The names, Jim Bridger, Peter Skein Ogden, Jedediah Smith, Etienne Provost and Hugh Glass, bring to mind strong, independent and rugged men who fearlessly lived in the Rocky Mountains. There, they traded with the Indian tribes, married the Indian women, trapped the rivers for beaver, and lived off the land. The legendary rendezvous, where Mountain Men gathered annually to trade furs for supplies and to eat, drink, tell stories and compete, has become as famous as the men themselves.

At Fort Buenaventura in Ogden, Utah, that exciting era is brought back to life. Guides in period dress interpret the lifestyle of the Mountain Men and the Indians who inhabited the area. Authentic artifacts are also displayed. Even the annual rendezvous is reenacted on special occasions. Fort Buenaventura has been recreated on the original site according to information found after much archeological and historical research. The actual fort was built in 1846 by Mountain Man, Miles Goodyear.

The current fort's dimensions, height of pickets, method of construction, and number and style of log cabins are all based on documented facts. There are no nails in the stockade; instead, wooden pegs and mortise and tenon joints hold the walls together.

Activites at the fort include guided tours, nature walks, canoeing, fishing, picnicking, horseshoes and volleyball. There are cabins to rent, a visitor center and a trading post.

Miles Goodyear & Fort Buenaventura

A change in hat styles – from beaver to silk – brought the fur trapping era to an end in 1840. This forced Mountain Men to look for other employment. Miles Goodyear decided to build Fort Buenaventura.

It was to be, as the Missouri Western Expositor explained in September, 1845, "a sort of halfway house between the East and Oregon and California, where the companies may stop and refresh themselves and obtain supplies."

The fort never served its intended purpose. In 1847, the Mormons settled Salt Lake Valley and purchased Goodyear's property on the Weber River. Under the Mormons, Fort Buenaventura was renamed Brownsville. It became the nucleus of settlements forming present-day Ogden.

For further information, contact Fort Buenaventura State Park, 2450 A Avenue, Ogden, UT 84401-2203. ☎ (801) 621-4808.

Fremont Indian State Park

Location: 21 miles southwest of Richfield on I-70 in central Utah.

Fremont Indian State Park was established to preserve Clear Creek Canyon's treasury of rock art and archeological sites. Visit the museum in the visitor center where a video program introduces you to the Fremont Indians. Three interpretive trails, one accessible to wheelchairs, lead you into legend and history depicted through pictographs and petroglyphs.

Fishing, hiking, camping and picnicking are available throughout the year.

For further information, contact Fremont Indian State Park, 11550 West Clear Creek Canyon Road, Sevier, UT 84766-9999. ☎ (801) 527-4631.

Goblin Valley State Park

Location: In Emery County between Green River and Hanksville. Follow Highway 24 to Temple Mountain Junction and proceed 14 miles southwest on a surfaced and improved gravel road.

Goblin Valley is Utah's skull in the sky, parade of elephants, and dance of the dolls. Unique and enchanting rock sculptures carved by wind and water suggest mischievous goblins of folklore still go about their secretive deeds. Add year-round solitude in a remote desert setting and you have the stuff dreams are made of. The antics of these goblins and balanced rocks, spires, and pedestals are limited only by your imagination.

Facilities

Facilities at the 3,654-acre park include a 21-unit campground, observation overlook, culinary water, modern restrooms, hot water showers, and sanitary dump station. Each spacious campsite has a picnic table, paved parking pad, and barbecue grill.

Area Attractions

Explore fascinating places from your Goblin Valley camp. Nearby landmarks include the Henry Mountains, San Rafael Reef and Swell, Temple Mountain, Molly's Castle, Gilsen Buttes, and Wild Horse Butte. Numerous rocks and coves offer unlimited hiking opportunities. The area is a photographer's paradise, and off-road enthusiasts will find many miles of dirt roads to explore. History buffs can discover traces of early Indians, prospectors, miners and ranchers.

Canyonlands National Park, Arches National Monument, Green River State Park, Dead Horse Point State Park, Glen Canyon National Recreation Area, and Capitol Reef National Park are within a two-hour drive.

Plants & Animals

Vegetation is limited to hardy desert species that can endure blowing sand and hot, dry surface conditions. You are likely to encounter Mormon tea (jointfir), wild onion, Russian thistle, Indian ricegrass, tumbleweed, shadscale, winterfat, larkspur and various cacti. Nearby, at slightly higher elevations, are juniper and pinyon pine. Fremont cottonwood trees are plentiful along streambeds.

Most animals in the area are nocturnal, venturing out only in the cooler evenings. Spotted skunks, porcupines, scorpions, chuchwalla lizards, kangaroo rats, kit foxes, coyotes, bobcats, jack rabbits, gophers, and badgers are found within and near the park.

Geology

Goblin Valley State Park is a showcase of geologic history. Exposed cliffs reveal parallel layers of rock bared by erosion. Because of the uneven hardness of sandstone, some patches resist erosion much better than others. The softer material is removed by wind and water, leaving thousands of unique, geologic "goblins." Water erosion and smoothing action of wind-blown dust work together to shape the goblins.

Bedrock is exposed because of thin soil and lack of vegetation. When rail does fall, there are few plant roots and little soil to capture and hold the water, which quickly disappears in muddy streams without penetrating the bedrock.

History

Secluded Goblin Valley was first discovered by cowboys searching for cattle. Then, in the late 1920's, Arthur Chaffin, owner/operator of the Hite ferry, and two companions were searching for an alternative route between Green River and Cainsville. They came to a vantage point about a mile west of Goblin Valley and were in awe at what they saw – five buttes and a valley of strange rock formations surrounded by a wall of eroded cliffs.

In 1949, Chaffin returned to the area he called Mushroom Valley. He spent several days exploring and photographing its strange shapes.

Publicity attracted visitors to the valley despite its remoteness. In 1954, it was proposed that Goblin Valley be protected from vandalism. The state of Utah later acquired the property and established Goblin Valley State Reserve. It was officially designated a state park on August 24, 1964.

Energy From the Sun

Facilities at Goblin Valley get their electricity from the sun's renewable energy. Photovoltaic (foe-toe-vol-tay-ik) cells convert sunlight directly to electricity for two ranger residences and the public restrooms.

Photovoltaic (PV) cells face south at an angle to collect as much energy as possible. When sunlight strikes them, direct current electricity (DC) is created. It is stored in large, deep cycle batteries housed in an adjacent building. A power inverter changes DC electricity into alternating currents (AC) electricity. The system stores enough power for three days without sunlight.

The 28 silicon PV cells at Goblin Valley form an arrangement called an array. Each one-by-four-foot cell produces 48 watts of power. The total system produces 1.4 kw. It replaces a 15 kw diesel-powered generator.

PV systems are cost-effective in remote locations where power demand is small and when there are no electric transmission lines. Solar energy is a noiseless, pollution-free source of electricity.

Goblin also uses the sun's energy to heat water for the park's public restrooms. Solar collectors on the roof absorb the sun's heat. Coils in back of the collectors are filled with antifreeze. The sun heats the antifreeze, which is then pumped into a heat exchanger where it heats water for showers and other uses. After the antifreeze releases its heat, it is returned to the solar collectors and the cycle begins again.

Culinary water for the park also is provided by energy from the sun. Solar panels collect energy to power a deep-well water pump. The pump supplies water to a 40,000 gallon storage tank that provides water for visitors and personnel. The solar panels are mounted on a movable rack that automatically follows the sun throughout the day to maximize the amount of energy tapped.

The solar energy systems were installed by the Utah Energy Office in partnership with the Utah Division of Parks and Recreation. They demonstrate how we can produce energy from renewable resources, and reduce fossil fuel consumption and related pollution.

For further information, contact Goblin Valley State Park, PO Box 637, Green River, UT 84525-0637. ☎ (801) 564-3633.

Goosenecks State Park

Location: 4 miles off UT 261, near Mexican Hat.

At Goosenecks you can look into a 1,000-foot-deep chasm carved through the Pennsylvania Hermosa Formation by the silt-laden San Juan River. The river meanders back and forth for more than five miles, traveling only one linear mile.

The access road is paved. Facilities include primitive camping and vault restrooms.

For further information, contact Goosenecks State Park, PO Box 788, Blanding, UT 84511-0788. ☎ (801) 678-2258.

Great Salt Lake State Park

Location: 16 miles west of Salt Lake City.

"Immediately at our feet we beheld the object of our anxious search, waters of the inland sea, stretching and still in solitary grandeur far beyond our vision" John C. Fremont, 1847

Imagine yourself lying on beautiful white sand beaches peering at miles and miles of open, tranquil sea. You might think you're on the Pacific Coast, but welcome to Utah's Great Salt Lake State Park, where recreation opportunities abound amidst panoramic grandeur. Enjoy your stay at the Great Salt Lake, a saline remnant of ancient Lake Bonneville.

America's Inland Sea

The Great Salt Lake is a large, inland body of water 40 miles wide and 80 miles long with no outlets. Its salt content varies from 3 to 27%, and many brackish estuaries border the terminal lake. The Great Salt Lake is quite literally America's inland sea.

History

In 1710 explorer Baron Lahoutan heard tales from native American Indians about a large, salty lake. In 1776 Father Escalante's exploration party camped at nearby Utah Lake. But no white explorers saw the Great Salt Lake until the winter of 1824-25 when Jim Bridger and his trapper brigade floated down the Bear River to its confluence with the lake. When Bridger tasted the salty water, he thought he had reached the Pacific Ocean. Later explorers circumnavigated the lake and discovered it had no outlets.

The Lake Wasn't Always Salty

Twenty thousand years ago fresh water filled the basins of northwest Utah with runoff from melting glaciers. Today's lake is a mere remnant of ancient Lake Bonneville, which was 2,000 feet deep and covered 20,000 square miles. Terraces on mountainsides adjacent to the Great Salt Lake are actually old beaches created by the pounding of ancient waves.

Utah's Salty Sea

Early pioneers marveled at the Great Salt Lake's high salt content and resulting buoyancy. The high salinity allows objects to "float like a cork."

The lake's salt content varies in relation to the amount of fresh water entering it. Freshwater streams carry large amounts of dissolved minerals into the lake. When the fresh water evaporates, a salty brine is left behind.

Life In & Around the Lake

Insects and brine shrimp are the only life forms that can thrive in the Great Salt Lake. The high salt content prohibits most forms of aquatic life from living there.

Five species of migratory birds use islands in the lake for spring and summer nesting, feeding on insects and brine shrimp. California gulls are abundant and, as they can survive on almost anything, don't have to leave the lake. However, herons, cormorants, terns, and pelicans are fish eaters and must migrate a hundred miles to find food. The lake's isolated islands are virtually predator free.

Other wildlife in the lake region includes squirrels, antelope, deer and wild ponies on Fremont Island, and buffalo on Antelope Island.

Natural Resources

The Great Salt Lake is a valuable natural resource. Mining, recreation, and wildlife must be managed wisely. Hundreds of thousands of tons of salt and other minerals are extracted from lake brine each year. Brine shrimp are harvested and sold halfway around the world. Shoreline marshes and isolated islands provide important wildlife habitat.

For further information, contact Great Salt Lake State Park, PO Box 323, Magna, UT 84044-0323. ☎ (801) 250-1898.

Green River State Park

Location: City limits of Green River.

At an elevation of 4,000 feet, Green River State Park is an oasis on the west bank of the Green River where tall cottonwood trees shade well-manicured lawns. The park is a favorite embarkation point for river trips and is a great base for seeing scenic southeast Utah. Within an hour's drive are Arches and Canyonlands national parks, Dead Horse Point and Goblin Valley state parks, and the San Rafael Reef. Park personnel can help you plan an outing that is just right for you and your family.

Special Features

Facilities at the 63-acre Green River State Park include a 42-unit campground, group-use facility, modern restrooms, hot showers, day-use area, small amphitheater for interpretive programs, sewage dump station, and a boat ramp. Each roomy campsite has a picnic table, paved parking pad, and barbecue grill.

Rafting

The Green River is one of Utah's premier river-running waters. North of the park the river winds its way through spectacular Desolation and Gray canyons where placid stretches of river are interrupted by churning, whitewater rapids. South of the park, the river meanders through the red rocks of Labyrinth Canyon. Further south, after the Green joins the Colorado, the mighty river fights its way through Cataract Canyon for some of the best white-water rafting in the United States.

Friendship Cruise

Each Memorial Day weekend, the 200-mile Friendship Cruise launches from Green River State Park. As many as 400 motor boats float down the Green River to its confluence with the Colorado River, then motor up the Colorado to Moab through majestic but lonely canyons. ☎ (801) 538-7221 for information.

Off-Highway Vehicles

The San Rafael Desert surrounding Green River State Park is an excellent area for riding off-road vehicles. Opportunities to explore this beautiful backcountry are unlimited.

Rockhounding

Hills and canyons within a few miles of the park are rich in rocks and minerals. Agate, jasper, petrified wood, geodes, and other minerals are plentiful. Keep your eyes open.

Crystal Geyser

Crystal Geyser is a rare, cold water geyser formed from an unsuccessful oil test well. It is five miles south of the park on the east bank of the Green River. The geyser erupts erratically now, but interesting mineral deposits are there to see at any time.

Plants & Animals

Cottonwood and Russian olive trees, willows, tamarisks, cattails, and salt grass vegetate the park. Birdwatchers will find long-term residents such as robins, kingfishers, and mourning doves alongside ibises, egrets, herons, hawks, owls and a variety of songbirds. Squirrels scurry up and down tree trunks while muskrats paddle up the small stream that runs through the park. Early risers may glimpse beavers swimming in the river.

Green River Melons

Green River City is famous for its melons. Each September the city celebrates Melon Days, drawing people from throughout the area. Activities include a fair and parade, games, races, exhibits, dances, and plenty of delicious Green River melons. ☎ (801) 538-7221 for information.

History

The rugged canyons carved out by the Green River were a mystery until 1869 when an expedition of geologists, geographers, scouts, and adventurers headed by Major John Wesley Powell floated the river from present-day Green River, Wyoming, to the mouth of the Grand Canyon in Arizona. Their goal was "to fill in the last white space on the map, to explore the last great unmapped and unknown part of the continental United States."

Powell discovered that he was not the first to explore the area. In 1836 French trapper, Denis Julien, had chipped his name into the rock walls of the canyon. Fremont Indian (a.d. 500-1200) petroglyphs can be spotted in cliffs along the river and in tributary canyons.

For further information, contact Green River State Park, PO Box 637, Green River, UT 84525-0637. ☎ (801) 564-3633.

Gunlock State Park

Location: 15 miles northwest of sunny St. George.

The 240-acre Gunlock Reservoir offers year-round water sports, boating and quality fishing for bass and catfish attract visitors. Facilities include boat launching ramp, primitive camping and pit privies.

For further information, contact Gunlock State Park, PO Box 140, Santa Clara, UT 84765-0140. ☎ (801) 628-2255.

Historic Union Pacific Rail Trail State Park

Location: Follows I-80 through Wanship and Coalville to Echo Reservoir.

This park is unique. The trail is nearly 30 miles long and averages 125 feet wide. It traverses an area rich in cultural history from the Wasatch Mountains near Park City, across wetland meadows in

Silver Creek Canyon, through the towns of Wanship and Coalville, and along the Weber River to Echo Reservoir. Whether biking, hiking, horseback riding, cross-country skiing or walking, you will enjoy the sights and sounds along the way.

Plants & Animals

In spring an fall you may see mule deer, elk and moose. Smaller animals include marmots (rock chuck), cottontail rabbits, red foxes and coyotes. Hawks and owls inhabit the area year-round, and sandhill cranes can be seen in open meadows during spring and summer. Songbirds flourish in willow, dogwood and wild rose thickets. Winter birdwatchers may see bald eagles roosting in cottonwood trees along the Weber River or near Echo Reservoir.

Berry pickers will find wild currants, chokecherries and service berries along the trail corridor. The area between Atkinson and Wanship is especially fruitful.

Archeology, Geology & Paleontology

Anyone interested in archeology, geology or paleontology will be intrigued by the rail trail in Summit County. Geologists say the Park City mining district is part of an extensive metallic mineral belt stretching west to the Oquirrh, Tintic and Deep Creek mountains. A 1960's excavation in the Silver Creek Junction area uncovered fossils of mammoths, sabertooth cats and other species more than 40,000 years old. The canyon between Silver Creek Junction and Wanship contains ancient volcanic deposits, and the Coalville area once resembled a swampy coastal plain. Long ago, sediments formed the coal deposits and red cliffs that surround Echo Reservoir.

Archeologists report evidence that Fremont Indians once inhabited Summit County. Bands of Ute and Shoshone Indians were encountered by fur trapper Etienne Provost in 1825. Provost and fellow trappers were among the first outsiders to enter Summit County.

Trail Access

Park City - When coming from Salt Lake City, take Exit 145 off I-80, turn right on Route 224 into Park City, then left on Kearns Boulevard (Route 248), right on Bonanza Drive, then turn left on Prospector Avenue. Parking is on your right, just beyond the plaza.

From US 40, take Exit 4 (Route 248) into Park City. Turn left on Bonanza Drive, then left on Prospector Avenue. Parking is on your right, just beyond Park City Plaza. The next trail access seven miles northeast.

Star Pointe - Trail access is located east of Silver Creek Industrial Park. Access is from US 40 at Silver Creek interchange. Next trail access seven miles northeast.

Wanship - Take Wanship Exit 156 off I-80. Parking is northeast of Spring Chicken Inn on Route 189. Next trail access is eight miles north.

Coalville - Take Coalville Exit 164 off I-80, bear right off the ramp and proceed left on Main Street. Turn left on 200 North. Next trail access five miles north.

Echo Reservoir - Limited parking. Future trail access to be located below and east of Echo Dam.

At its northern end, the rail trail intersects with the Mormon Pioneer National Historic Trail. The Mormon pioneers followed this route in 1847 from Nauvoo, Illinois to Salt Lake City, Utah.

Railroad History

In 1869, Coalville-Echo Railroad Company was hired to transport coal five miles from the Coalville mines to the Union Pacific line at Echo. Due to a shortage of track, plans were abandoned. Increasing demand for coal prompted citizens to reorganize in 1871. They emerged as the Summit County Railroad Company. By 1873, coal was moving from Coalville to the Wasatch Front on a narrow-gauge track.

Meanwhile, silver was discovered in the Park City Mountains. Coal was needed to fuel the pumps that removed water from underground mines. Utah Eastern Railroad was organized in 1879 to build a narrow-gauge line between Coalville and Park City. Union Pacific Railroad began constructing a broad-gauge spur line, Echo-Park City Railway. Both lines were completed in 1880.

Competition from Union Pacific proved too much for local companies. Within three years, the narrow-gauge railroad was out of business. Union Pacific Railroad served the Park City area for another 100 years. The Phoston Spur was added during this time, serving the silver and phosphate mine in Wasatch County.

As the number of operating mines decreased in Coalville and Park City, the need for a railroad also dwindled. Passenger service to entice skiers to Park City was tried and discontinued during the mid 1970's. Freight service ended 10 year later.

In 1989, Union Pacific Railroad abandoned the railroad line from Echo to Park City and Phoston Spur. The Utah Division of Parks and Recreation, A & K Railroad Materials and Union Pacific Railroad launched plans to turn the abandoned railroad corridor into a non-motorized recreation trail. After removing the rails and ties, A & K Railroad Materials donated the rail corridor to the Utah Division of Parks and Recreation.

The Historic Union Pacific Rail Trail State Park was dedicated on October 3, 1992. It is the first non-motorized rail trail in Utah.

Guidelines

The rail trail is shared by pedestrians, cyclists, equestrians and cross-country skiers. Please observe the following guidelines to ensure that everyone's visit is pleasant:

- Bring your own water; none is available on the trail.
- Be prepared for Utah's dramatic weather changes.
- Carry out more than you carry in. Leave no trace.
- Pedestrians should yield to equestrians.

- Motorized vehicles are prohibited on the rail trail (except for maintenance, law enforcement and emergency vehicles).
- Close all gates behind you.
- Firearms and fireworks are not permitted.

Cyclists:

- Yield to other trail users. A friendly word makes a good impression. Make enough sound to avoid surprising hikers.
- Ride at a safe, controlled speed and wear protective head gear and clothing.
- Carry repair tools, at least a tire patch kit and air pump.

Cyclists and Equestrians:

- If overtaking a horse from behind, make your presence known and ask to pass. It may take a moment for the rider to find a safe place to stop. Talk calmly to reassure the horse, and ride or walk your bicycle slowly.
- Keep in mind that any horse can spook. If the horse shows signs of spooking, get off your bicycle and stand quietly out of the horse's path. Avoid making sudden movements or loud noises.

Private Property and Pets:

- A large percentage of the rail trail is surrounded by private land. Please stay on the trail and respect the rights of private landowners.
- Pets are allowed but must be confined on a maximum six-foot leash. Ranchers have the right to shoot free-roaming animals that bother grazing stock. Please keep your pets under control.

For further information, contact Historic Union Pacific Rail Trail State Park, PO Box 309, Heber City, UT 84032-0309. ☎ (801) 645-8036.

Huntington State Park

Location: In Emery County, 2 miles north of Huntington and 20 miles south of the city of Price. Follow State Highway 10 to the well-signed turnoff and travel a quarter-mile west on a paved road to the park entrance.

Picture yourself relaxing on lush, green grass, shaded by trees. Beside you lies a peaceful reservoir. Close by are beautifully landscaped picnic areas and campground spaces. Where are you? Huntington State Park in scenic Castle Valley.

Special Features

Facilities at Huntington State Park include a spacious, 22-unit campground, numerous picnic sites, covered group pavilion with picnic tables, drinking water, modern restrooms, hot water showers, sanitary dump station, boat ramp and boat docks, and swimming beaches. Each campsite has a picnic table, barbecue grill, paved parking pad, and lawn area for tents.

Activities

A host of water-related activities await. The boat ramp provides access for all types of watercraft. Warm water makes the reservoir extremely popular for waterskiing. Swimming beaches are a favorite for children. Service roads around the reservoir provide two miles of scenic hiking and jogging trails.

Off-highway vehicles are not allowed to unload in the park. However, a 10-minute drive west takes you to an outstanding mountain riding area, and a 15-minute drive east puts you on the edge of the San Rafael Swell for superb desert riding. Perhaps the most popular activity at Huntington State Park, though, is just plain relaxing.

Fishing

Huntington Reservoir is one of Utah's finer warm-water fisheries. Particularly noteworthy are largemouth bass. Some good bluegill fishing can also be found here. And crawdad fishing is popular, especially with children. Be sure to check the fishing regulations.

Because of its oasis nature, the park is frequented by many migrating birds, particularly waterfowl.

Area Attractions

Your Huntington State Park campsite is an excellent jumping off point for exploring Utah's most extraordinary scenery. High mountain meadows and streams, deep desert canyons, Indian petroglyphs, the world's most productive dinosaur quarry, three museums, and lofty view points are all within an hour's drive of the park. Park personnel can help you plan an outing.

History

The reservoir at Huntington State Park was completed in 1966. The US Bureau of Reclamation built it as part of an Emery County irrigation and recreation project. The shore area has since been managed as a state park.

For further information, contact Huntington State Park, PO Box 1343, Huntington, UT 84528-1343. ☎ (801) 687-2491.

Hyrum State Park

Location: City limits of Hyrum.

Hyrum State Park invites boating, year-round fishing, waterskiing, camping, and swimming on a 450-acre lake in northern Utah. Attractions less than 15 minutes from the park include Utah State University, a Mormon temple, and scenic mountains. Hardware Ranch (winter wildlife feeding ranch) is 16 miles from the park up beautiful Blacksmith Fork Canyon.

For further information, contact Hyrum State Park, 405 West 300 South, Hyrum, UT 84319-1547. ☎ (801) 245-6866.

Iron Mission State Park

Location: Center of Cedar City.

The Iron Mission Story

Lack of iron was a major concern to pioneers who began settling in Utah in 1847. When iron deposits were discovered in southern Utah, Mormon leader Brigham Young called for volunteers to colonize the Iron Mission area. A site near Coal Creek (Cedar City) was selected in November 1851 for the iron works. Ten months later the colony completed construction of a small blast furnace and began to operate the iron foundry.

Despite its initial success, the Iron Mission faced many difficulties. Indian troubles, floods, heavy freezes, and furnace failure took their toll. In addition, a crop shortage threatened starvation. The people persevered in the face of these obstacles, but the foundry eventually closed in 1858.

A diorama based on descriptions of the original foundry is on display at the park.

Horse-Drawn Vehicle Collection

Pioneer diversity is the cornerstone of the museum's horse-drawn vehicle collection gathered from widely scattered Utah farms and towns. Begun by Mr. Gronway Parry in 1911, the unique collection includes vehicles used from 1870 to 1930.

Intriguing coaches and wagons include a bullet-scarred overland stage from Butch Cassidy's era in the Four Corners area and a recreation of a legendary Wells Fargo stagecoach. Standing in sharp contrast are the Stanhope Phaeton, forerunner of today's compact car, and an original Studebaker White Top Wagon, predecessor of the present-day station wagon.

You will find buggies, surreys, mail carts, horse-drawn farm machinery, an old milk wagon, a hearse, and even a "one-horse open sleigh." Industrial vehicles such as dump-belly and freight wagons, a low-wheeled dray, and a water sprinkling wagon are also on display. Each vehicle in the collection has played an important role in Utah life.

Indian Artifacts

Some 200 Indian relics, including articles of clothing, hunting weapons, and food processing tools, make up the William R. Palmer Collection. These artifacts were once used by Southern Paiutes in southwestern Utah, southern Nevada, and northern Arizona.

The Paiutes were a nomadic people who moved about the area in search of food. Their simple diet consisted mainly of seeds, insects, and small game.

The Southern Paiutes formally adopted William R. Palmer into their tribe in 1926 to acknowledge his sympathetic research and understanding.

Hours

The museum is open daily except Thanksgiving, Christmas, and New Year's Day. Winter hours (Labor Day to Memorial Day) are 9 am to 5 pm. Summer hours are 9 am to 7 pm. A picnic area is available, but there is no camping.

For further information, contact Iron Mission State Park, PO Box 1079, 585 North Main, Cedar City, UT 84720-1079. ☎ (801) 586-9290.

Jordan River State Park

Location: 1700 South in Salt Lake City to the Davis County line.

Whether you're a canoeist, jogger, golfer, or picnicker, Jordan River State has something for you. Recreation developments run north along an 8½-mile corridor of the Jordan River from 1700 South in Salt Lake City to the Davis County line.

Park activities include canoe and float opportunities with various put-in and take-out points; restrooms and picnic areas at 1700 South, 800 South, and Cottonwood Park; 1¼-mile jogging/exercise course; handicap exercise course; walking and bicycle trail;

modelport; nine-hole, par-three golf course, and an off-road vehicle riding area.

For further information, contact Jordan River State Park, 1084 North Redwood Road, Salt Lake City, UT 84720-1079. ☎ (801) 533-4496 (office); (801) 533-4527 (golf course).

Jordanelle State Park

Location: 6 miles north of Heber.

Jordanelle Reservoir is located in a picturesque mountain setting near Heber City, Utah. It is Utah's newest state park, still under construction, and will provide boating, camping, and picnicking.

Hailstone, set on the west shore of the reservoir off US 40, opened in the spring of 1995. Facilities will include 230 developed campsites, modern restrooms, showers, laundry, utility hookups, sewage disposal station, visitor center, sandy beaches, group-use pavilions, sun shelter, 80-slip marina with utility hookups, fuel dispensing, general store, and restaurant. The park will also have three play areas and miles of trails for non-motorized vehicles.

Rock Cliff, on the Provo River two miles west of Francis on SR 32, opened in the spring of 1994. Facilities include an elevated nature center, boardwalks, 50 walk-in camping sites, group use area, modern restrooms, showers, and a small boat access ramp.

Contact Jordanelle State Park, PO Box 309, Heber City, UT 84032-0309. ☎ (801) 645-8036.

Kodachrome Basin State Park

Location: 9 miles south of State Route 12 near Cannonville.

Kodachrome Basin is a spectacle of massive sandstone chimneys. Numerous rocks and coves offer solitude, quiet, and unique desert beauty. Nearby attractions include Bryce Canyon National Park, Grosvenor Arch, Paria Canyon, movie sets and ghost town remains.

Overnight camping facilities, drinking water, modern restrooms, hot showers, and sewage disposal station are available. An area with picnic tables, fire pit, barbecue grills, and electricity is great for group outings. A concessionaire provides horse rentals. The park has a resident ranger.

For further information, contact Kodachrome Basin State Park, PO Box 238, Cannonville, UT 84718-0238. ☎ (801) 679-8562.

Lost Creek State Park

Location: 10 miles northeast of Croyden.

Located in the forested mountains of northern Utah, Lost Creek is a perfect boating, fishing and water sports retreat. Facilities include a boat launching ramp, primitive camping, pit privies, and trash removal.

For further information, contact Lost Creek State Park, 5535 South Highway 66, Morgan, UT 84050-9694. ☎ (801) 829-6866.

Millsite State Park

Location: 4 miles west of Ferron.

Would you like to visit a secret getaway? One where you can relax amid a beautiful, uncrowded array of amenities and recreation opportunities? Millsite State Park is just such a place.

At an elevation of 6,100 feet, Millsite State Park is in southeastern Utah's Emery County at the mouth of scenic Ferron Canyon, four miles west of Ferron. Majestic cliffs that tower 2,000 feet directly above the 435-acre reservoir provide an impressive setting for fun and relaxation.

Special Features

Facilities at Millsite State Park include 20 shoreline campsites, several picnic sites, two large covered group pavilions with picnic tables and fire pits, drinking water, modern restrooms with hot showers, a sanitary disposal station, boat ramp and boat docks, and a sandy beach. The campground has lawn areas for tents. Each campsite has a level parking pad, picnic table, and barbecue grill.

Activities

Millsite State Park is a great vacation destination. Visitors come to camp, picnic, fish, swim, sail, waterski, relax, sunbathe, and enjoy the quiet, panoramic Millsite Reservoir. Fishing from boat or shoreline may net prime cutthroat and rainbow trout.

Off-highway vehicles are not allowed in the park. However, a short drive to the west takes you to an outstanding mountain riding area, and a 15-minute drive east puts you on the edge of the San Rafael Swell for superb desert riding. The surrounding area provides unlimited hiking and mountain biking opportunities. To top it all off, Ferron City's challenging nine-hole Millsite Golf Course is adjacent to the park.

Plants & Animals

Most of the developed park area is landscaped with lawns and hybrid popular trees. A large natural section contains desert plants with a nature trail and signs that inform you of the types of vegetation.

The park is situated within the wintering grounds of some of Utah's largest big game herds. Winter visitors enjoy ice fishing and a potential look at deer, elk, and moose.

Nearby Points of Interest

Your Millsite State Park campsite is an excellent starting point for exploration. High mountain meadows and streams, deep desert canyons, the world's most productive dinosaur quarry, three museums, and lofty view points are all within an hour's drive of the park. Particularly noteworthy is the park's proximity to some of the country's most outstanding Indian rock art panels, which may be centuries old.

History

Millsite Reservoir was completed in 1970. The US Soil Conservation Service built the reservoir to retain water and add to the recreational opportunities in the area. The shore area has been managed as a state park since 1971.

For further information, contact Millsite State Park, PO Box 1343, Huntington, UT 84528-1343. ☎ (801) 687-2491.

Minersville State Park

Location: 13 miles southwest of Beaver, Utah, off State Route 21.

Minersville is in southwest Utah near the Tushar and Mineral mountains. A developed campground and boating facilities enhance the recreation on and around the 1,130-acre Minersville Reservoir. The park sits at an elevation of 5,513 feet.

Special Features

Facilities include a 29-unit campground, modern restrooms with showers, sewage disposal and fish cleaning stations, launching ramp and boat docks. Each campsite has a picnic table, barbecue grill, water and electric hookups and paved parking. There is a large overflow area for primitive camping.

Activities

A host of water-related activities await you at Minersville State Park. The wide, concrete boat ramp provides access for all types of watercraft. Camping, picnicking, waterskiing, swimming, sunbathing, birdwatching and waterfowl hunting in season are popular pastimes.

Minersville Reservoir is one of Utah's prime fisheries. Particularly noteworthy are rainbow trout, cutthroat and smallmouth bass.

Hundreds of miles of desert and mountain trails are within a short driving distance. Off-highway riding is not permitted.

The surrounding area provides mountain lake and stream fishing, hiking, rockhounding, mountain biking, skiing and snowmobiling. Gasoline, food and other supplies can be purchased in nearby towns of Beaver, Minersville and Milford.

Plants & Animals

Sagebrush and wild grass dominate Minersville's vegetation. Cottonwoods and willows grow near the water with juniper and pinyon pines in the foothills.

Numerous wildlife species live in the area. Mammals include cougars, coyotes, jackrabbits, mule deer, skunks and squirrels. Many species of birds, insects and reptiles also inhabit the park.

History

On May 17, 1859, a group of settlers arrived at Beaver Creek to mine silver and lead. The area later was named Minersville. Several dams were built upstream to store irrigation water. They each washed away until Delta Land and Water Company completed the existing dam in 1914.

For further information, contact Minersville State Park, PO Box 1531, Beaver, UT 84713-1531. ☎ (801) 438-5472.

Otter Creek State Park

Location: 4 miles northwest of Antimony on State Route 22.

Fishing and boating on 3,120-acre Otter Creek Reservoir are the featured activities. Camping and picnicking units, modern restrooms with hot showers, fish cleaning and sewage disposal stations, boat launching ramp, and courtesy docks are available.

For further information, contact Otter Creek State Park, PO Box 1531, Beaver, UT 84713-1531. ☎ (801) 624-3268.

Palisade State Park

Location: 5 miles south of Manti.

Welcome to Palisade State Park, a great place for you and your family to relax and get away from it all. Nestled in a beautiful little valley in Sanpete County, the park is easily accessible. At an elevation of 5,868 feet, Palisade State Park's picturesque surroundings add a relaxing dimension to golfing, fishing, and ice skating.

Activities & Facilities

Summer activities include camping, fishing, swimming, non-motorized boating, golfing, hiking, and sunbathing on the sandy beach. If you're a winter enthusiast, try ice fishing, cross-country skiing, ice skating, or a winter golf tournament.

The golf course has some of the best putting greens in the state. A PGA professional provides a full range of services and all supplies can be found at the pro shop. Meals and camping supplies are also available at the clubhouse.

There are 53 individual campsites along with two group-use areas. Modern restrooms with hot water showers, culinary water, and a sewage dump station are also available.

In nearby Sixmile Canyon, you can hike, hunt in season, or ride your four-wheel-drive vehicle. Twelvemile Canyon claims some of the largest quaking aspen trees in the region at Grove of the Giant Aspens. Skyline Drive takes you on a 10,000-foot-high drive along the crest of the spectacular Wasatch Plateau.

Plants & Animals

Within the park you will enjoy grass, cottonwood and spruce trees. The surrounding area is of a semi-arid terrain with juniper and pinyon pine trees. Sagebrush, rabbit brush, and low-growing cactus also grow throughout the area. Native grasses and wildflowers fill in the open spaces.

In summer, rock chucks, squirrels, and hares are common on the lower slopes. Birds include flickers, kingfishers, hawks, jays, and swallows. A favorite sighting is the beautiful Western tanager. From fall through spring, you will probably see the many mule deer, bald eagle, great blue heron, and a number of migratory waterfowl that inhabit the area.

History

Funk's Lake, as it was then known, was created in 1873 by an enterprising pioneer named Daniel B. Funk. He wanted surrounding settlers to have a place to relax. At that time this small valley was "owned" by a small group of Sanpitch Indians led by Chief Arapeen. Mr. Funk bargained with the chief and obtained a land patent from the government. Then he set about the arduous task of building an earthen dam and diverting part of Sixmile Creek to fill the lake. The lake quickly became a well-known pleasure resort.

For further information, contact Palisade State Park, PO Box H, Manti, UT 84642-0076. ☎ (801) 835-7275 (office); (801) 835-4653 (golf course).

Pioneer Trail State Park

Location: Near the city zoo, east on Sunnyside Avenue.

Take a walk into the past at Pioneer Trail State Park. Old Deseret is a living history museum that recreates a typical community between 1847 and 1869. Structures include adobe houses, shops, public buildings, and the restored Brigham Young Forest Farmhouse with period furnishings and artifacts. Pioneer Trail State Park is Utah's most renowned historic park. It is on the east bench of Salt Lake City at the mouth of Emigration Canyon.

The Place Monument, south of Old Deseret, was erected in 1947. It is on the National Register and commemorates the 100th anniversary of the arrival of Mormon pioneers to the Salt Lake Valley. Early Spanish explorers, Mountain Men, and native Americans also are featured. An audio presentation and three-wall mural portraying the 1,300-mile migration of Mormon pioneers from Nauvoo, Illinois to the Great Salt Lake Valley are featured at the visitor center. Picnic areas are available.

For further information, contact Pioneer Trail State Park, 2601 Sunnyside Avenue, Salt Lake City, UT 84108-1453. ☎ (801) 584-8391.

Piute State Park

Location: 12 miles south of Marysvale just off US Highway 89.

Piute State Park and its 3,360-acre mountain lake are open year-round for trophy fishing. Popular activities include camping, boating, rockhounding, and waterfowl hunting in season. Facilities are limited.

For further information, contact Piute State Park, PO Box 43, Antimony, UT 84712-0043. ☎ (801) 624-3268.

Quail Creek State Park

Location: 3 miles east of the I-15 Hurricane exit on State Route 9.

Quail Creek State Park provides excellent year-round camping, picnicking, boating, and trout and bass fishing in southwest Utah. Facilities include 23 campsites, modern restrooms, fish cleaning station, and two group-use pavilions.

For further information, contact Quail Creek State Park, PO Box 1943, St. George, UT 84770-1943. ☎ (801) 879-2378.

Red Fleet State Park

Location: In the heart of Dinosaurland, 10 miles north of Vernal Utah on Highway 191.

The park's name was inspired by three large Navajo sandstone outcrops that jut up from the water, resembling a fleet of ships. At an elevation of 5,600 feet, Red Fleet offers camping, picnicking, swimming, fishing and boating. Nearby attractions take in Dinosaur National Monument, Flaming Gorge National Recreation Area, Steinaker and Utah Field House of Natural History state parks, and rafting and fishing on the Green River.

Special Features

Facilities include 31 campsites with side-by-side parking, modern restrooms, barbecue grills, covered picnic tables, a concrete boat launching ramp, and stations for sewage disposal and fish cleaning. The park has a resident ranger. The campground sits on a hillside that provides a panoramic view of the reservoir and surrounding area. Its design is different from most campgrounds. There is a central parking area. Individual tables and fire pits are a short distance away on the grass. Camping is available on a first-come, first-served basis.

Activities

Local boaters refer to the 650-acre Red Fleet Reservoir as Little Lake Powell. Spectacular sandstone cliffs and secluded sandy beaches await visitors who love water-oriented activities. You can launch your boat for a day of fishing and waterskiing or hike to an isolated beach for picnicking and swimming. Swimmers should use caution, however, as the water may be extremely deep just off shore.

Red Fleet Reservoir is one of Utah's prime fisheries. Particularly noteworthy are rainbow and brown trout, bluegill and bass.

Dinosaur Tracks

Dinosaurs crossed this area 190 to 200 million years ago. They left footprints in the mud and damp sand along the shoreline of a small desert lake. The footprints now are preserved in the rock immediately across the reservoir from the boat ramp. You may boat across or walk in from the north to view the footprints. Contact a ranger for directions and the best viewing area.

Disturbing or removing rock from this area is prohibited. Please leave the dinosaur footprints for other visitors to enjoy.

Plants & Animals

Juniper, sagebrush, native grasses and cactus dominate the area. Red Fleet is home to mammals such as rabbits, ground squirrels, bobcat, badger, coyote and mule deer. On cold mornings, golden eagles are often seen sunning themselves on the sandstone ridges.

Other birds include magpies, hawks, bluebirds, vultures, owls and an occasional osprey.

For further information, contact Red Fleet State Park, 4335 North Highway 191, Vernal, UT 84078-7800. ☎ (801) 789-4432.

Rockport State Park

Location: 45 miles east of Salt Lake City near Wanship on State Route 32.

R ockport Reservoir features first-rate fishing, waterskiing, swimming and sailboating. Nine campgrounds offer both developed and primitive camping in a variety of settings. A cross-country ski trail is available during the winter and ice fishing also is popular. A concessionaire provides boat rentals and other supplies.

For further information, contact Rockport State Park, 9040 North State Highway 302, Peoa, UT 84061-9702. ☎ (801) 336-2241.

Scofield State Park

Location: In Carbon County on State Route 96, just 10 miles south of Colton Junction.

S ituated in a valley in the Manti-LaSal Mountains, Scofield State Park is a popular destination for boaters, anglers and camping enthusiasts. The reservoir covers 2,800 acres at an elevation of 7,616 feet.

The park is open May through November. The reservoir is accessible year-round.

Special Features

Mountain View, six miles north of the town of Scofield, provides a grand view of the reservoir with towering mountains in the background. Facilities include a 34-unit campground, drinking water, modern restrooms, hot showers, group day-use pavilion, fish cleaning and sewage disposal stations and boat ramp. Each campsite has a picnic table, barbecue grill and parking pad.

Madsen Bay, on the north end of the reservoir, is a popular area for groups and familes. Facilities include a 40-unit campground, drinking water, modern restrooms, group-use pavilion, boat ramp, docks, parking lot, and sanitary disposal and fish cleaning stations. A forested tent-camping area and a wildlife interpretive section are a short distance away.

Lakeside day-use area provides modern restrooms, group-use pavilion, grills and a boat dock accessible to handicapped visitors as well as a fishing platform.

Activities

Two boat launching ramps provide access for all types of watercraft. Camping, picnicking, waterskiing, swimming, hiking, photography and watching wildlife are popular activities.

Scofield Reservoir is one of Utah's prime year-round fisheries. Cool waters are ideal for rainbow and cutthroat trout. Below Scofield Dam, a footbridge leads to hiking and fishing areas along Lower Fish Creek.

The Mauti-LaSal National Forest offers hiking, mountain biking, off-road driving and horseback riding. During winter, the area is a base for snowmobiling and cross-country skiing in the spectacular mountains surrounding the park.

History

Settlers came to Pleasant Valley in the 1870's to make use of the large tracts of grazing land. Forest industry developed in the adjacent mountains. The town of Scofield was named after General Charles W. Scofield, a timber contractor who became president of the state's first coal mining company.

Mining peaked in the early 1920's when Scofield had 12 stores, 13 saloons, four large hotels, a post office and a population of more than 6,000 residents. Today, less that 100 people live in the town.

Scofield always will be remembered for the most serious mine disaster in United States history. On May 1, 1900, the No. 4 mine in Winter Quarters Canyon exploded and claimed the lives of 199 men. There were not enough caskets in Utah to bury the dead.

Additional caskets had to be ordered from Denver. The weathered tombstones in the cemetery on the hill east of town give testimony of the tragedy.

Scofield Valley has experienced at least four separate dam efforts. In the early 1940's the existing earth-fill dam was completed. It is 128 feet high and backs more than 73,600 acre-feet of water.

For further information, contact Scofield State Park, PO Box 166, Price, UT 84501-0166. ☎ (801) 448-9449 (Summer); (801) 637-8497 (Winter).

Starvation State Park

Location: 4 miles west of Duchesne, Utah, just off US Highway 40.

Starvation State Park is a popular getaway for those who enjoy fishing, camping, water activities or just relaxing on a sandy beach. A developed campground and boating facilities enhance the recreation on and around the 3,495-acre Starvation Reservoir. The park sits at an elevation of 5,720 feet.

The Starvation Dam was completed in 1970. The US Bureau of Reclamation built the reservoir as part of the Central Utah Project. The shore has been managed as a state park since 1972.

Special Features

Starvation Reservoir offers 23 miles of shoreline for recreational pleasure. Five camping areas with facilities ranging from primitive to developed are located around the reservoir.

The Mountain View Campground, which overlooks the reservoir with the majestic Unita Mountains in the background, has 30 individual campsites with covered shelters. The Beach Campground has 24 grass sites and is popular for tent camping. Each developed site has a concrete parking pad, picnic table and barbecue grill. Other facilities include restrooms with hot showers, culinary water, sandy beach, picnic area, boat ramp, and fish cleaning and sewage disposal stations. A large covered pavilion with barbecue grills is popular for family reunions and group outings.

Four primitive campgrounds are scattered around the reservoir. Primitive campgrounds have vault toilets, but there is no culinary water available.

Activities

The wide, concrete boat launching camp provides access for all types of watercraft. Park visitors enjoy swimming and sunbathing on the developed sandy beach.

Starvation Reservoir is one of the Utah's best fishing areas for walleye. Other species found here include smallmouth bass and brown trout.

Off-Highway Vehicles

The Knight Hollow Primitive Camping Area provides 100 acres of sandy hills for off-road riding. To ensure a safe and enjoyable OHV experience, pay special attention to the following laws:

- Properly registered OHVs may be operated only in the Knight Hollow area designated open to OHV use.
- Properly-fitted, safety-rated helmets must be worn by OHV drivers and passengers under 18 years of age. All drivers and passengers of any age should wear protective head gear.
- No one under eight years of age may operate an OHV on public lands.
- Operators eight through 15 years of age must possess an OHV education certificate issued by the Utah Division of Parks and Recreation.

For more information, contact the ranger or call Utah Division of Parks and Recreation, OHV Information Center, at ☎ 800-OHV-RIDE.

Plants & Animals

Starvation State Park abounds with natural diversity. Juniper, pinyon and sagebrush dominate the landscape.

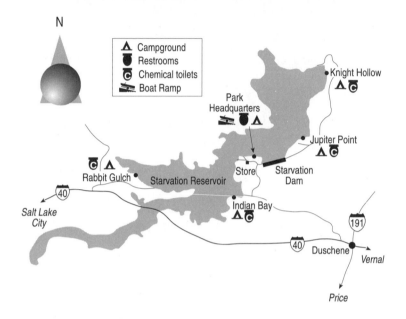

A variety of wildlife species can be found living in the park. Mammals include mule deer, cottontails, jack rabbits, beavers, badgers, chipmunks and prairie dogs. Coyotes, foxes, bobcats and elk are seen occasionally.

Birds common to the area include mountain bluebird, scrub jay, magpie and sparrows. Great blue herons, loons, Canadian geese and an assortment of ducks also frequent the park. A variety of hawks and an occasional golden or bald eagle may be seen.

For further information, contact Starvation State Park, PO Box 584, Duchesne, UT 84021-0584. ☎ (801) 738-2326.

Steinaker State Park

Location: 7 miles north of Vernal, Utah, off State Highway 191

Steinaker State Park is a desert oasis in the heart of Dinosaurland. Visitors come to fish, water ski, camp, picnic or relax on the beach. It sits at an elevation of 5,520 feet.

Steinaker is a good base camp to explore the attractions of Dinosaurland. Within a short driving distance are Flaming Gorge National Recreation Area, Ashley National Forest, Dinosaur National Monument, Red Fleet and Utah Field House of Natural History state parks, and the Green River.

Special Features

When full, Steinaker Reservoir covers 750 surface acres and is 130 feet deep in spots. Facilities at the 1,250-acre park include a 31-unit campground, modern restrooms, sewage disposal station, two group-use pavilions, sandy beaches and swim areas, self-guided nature trail, boat ramp and courtesy docks. Each campsite has a picnic table, paved parking pad, barbecue gill and fire pit.

Activities

Whether you fancy power boats, sail boards or canoes, Steinaker has it. Sandy beaches and water temperatures reaching 70°F in July make the park a water-lover's paradise. The concrete boat launching ramp provides access for all types of watercraft. To ensure a safe and enjoyable boating experience, pick up a copy of *Highlights from Utah Boating Laws and Rules* at the entrance station.

Steinaker Reservoir offers excellent fishing. You will find rainbow trout, large mouth bass and an occasional brown trout.

Geology

The surrounding area intrigues those interested in geology, paleontology or archeology. From high points in the park, you can see millions of years of geologic formations. A bank of the Morrison Formation runs along the east shore of the reservoir. This layer of strata was deposited 13 million years ago during the Jurassic Period when dinosaurs inhabited the area. The layer of rock may contain dinosaur fossils.

Plants & Animals

Juniper and sagebrush dominate Steinaker's vegetation. Cottonwoods and aspen grow near the water. In spring the park blooms with wildflowers, including larkspur, penstemon, Indian paintbrush and Utah's state flower, the sego lily.

Mammals found here include mule deer, jack rabbits, cottontails, porcupines and ground squirrels. Elk, coyotes and bobcats make rare appearances. Common birds are magpies, robins, scrub jays, pheasants, western grebes, loons, various ducks, Canada geese, turkey vultures, ospreys and golden eagles.

For further information, contact Steinaker State Park, 4335 North Highway 191, Vernal, UT 84078-7800. ☎ (801) 789-4432.

Territorial Statehouse State Park

Location: 50 West Capitol Avenue, off the I-15 Business Loop in Fillmore.

*U*tah's oldest existing government building is the Territorial Statehouse in Fillmore. Today, the statehouse is a museum that houses Utah pioneer artifacts and paintings. The collection includes butter churns, spinning wheels, firearms, farming equipment, woodworking tools, kitchen implements, clothing and many formal portraits. Furniture from pioneer homes is arranged in a variety of settings.

Upstairs in the legislative hall are paintings by pioneer and contemporary artists of Utah. Among these are works by Donald Beauregard, a Fillmore native. Beauregard began his studies in Utah and continued at the Academie Julian in Paris. An untimely death before his 30th birthday cut short a promising career.

An All American Rose Society garden and a shady picnic area adjoin the museum. Two restored pioneer cabins and a 1867 rock schoolhouse also fill the museum grounds. Clear Lake Wildlife

Refuge, Cove Fort and Chalk Creek Canyon are within short driving distances.

Utah's First Capital

In October 1851, Brigham Young headed a delegation of lawmakers representing the provisional State of Deseret. Their goal was to determine a locations for the capital city. A centrally located site 150 miles south of Salt Lake City was selected. The delegation named the city Fillmore in honor of Millard Fillmore, 13th president of the United States.

When the petition for statehood was denied, a territorial government was established. Brigham Young was appointed governor of the Utah Territory, and Fillmore became the territorial capital.

Construction of the Territorial Statehouse began in 1852. The original building plans called for three levels and four wings, connected by a Moorish dome at the center. Due to lack of funding, only the existing south wing was completed.

The territorial legislature met there in December 1855. This was the only full session held in the statehouse. The seat of government was returned to Salt Lake City in 1858.

Statehouse Restoration

The statehouse served a variety of purposes after 1858. It functioned as a civic center, religious meeting house, school, theater and jail. By the turn of the century the building had fallen into disuse and decay and was threatened with demolition.

In the mid 1920's the Daughters of the Utah Pioneers proposed the statehouse be restored as a museum. Under the direction of the Utah State Park and Recreation Commission, the museum opened in 1930 and was placed in custodial care of the Daughters of the Utah Pioneers.

Territorial Statehouse and grounds became a state park in 1957. It is listed on both the State and National Register of Historic Places.

Hours

The statehouse is open daily except Thanksgiving, Christmas and New Year's Day. Winter hours (Labor Day to Memorial Day) are 9 am to 6 pm.

For further information, contact 50 West Capitol, PO Box 657, Fillmore, UT 84631. ☎ (801) 743-5316.

Utah Field House of Natural History State Park

Location: In the heart of Dinosaurland in Vernal.

There are monsters in those mountains! And you can see them at the Utah Field House of Natural History State Park, a showcase of eastern Utah's geologic past and natural history. The field house, situated in downtown Vernal, is strategically placed between the Uinta Mountains (the largest single east-west range in the Western hemisphere) and the Uinta Basin (a petroleum-rich, intermountain valley). Together, these two features encompass almost three billion years of earth history. Their fossil record covers more than 600 million years and includes all forms of life from primitive algae to highly advanced mammals.

Special Features

The main features of the park are the museum and the dinosaur garden. The museum introduces you to the vast wealth of geology, paleontology, Indian prehistory, and natural history of the area. In addition to exhibits, it maintains a specimen collection for future displays, educational programs, and research. The museum also houses a small gift shop, science reference library, and classroom.

The dinosaur garden features 14 lifesize models of prehistoric animals in their natural setting. The sculptor, Elbert Porter, created the giant models, and Utah bought them in 1977. The garden is the combined effort of the local community and the Utah Division of Parks and Recreation. A group of three concrete dinosaurs by sculptor Millard F. Malin completes the outside display. In the summer, evening lectures are held in the garden amphitheater.

Area Attractions

In addition to Dinosaur National Monument with its dinosaur quarry and spectacular canyonlands, you may want to visit Ashley National Forest, the High Uinta Wilderness Area, the Green and Yampa rivers, Flaming Gorge National Recreation Area, the Book Cliffs, or the Ute Indian Reservation. Steinaker and Red Fleet state parks are just north of Vernal off US Highway 191. Both of these parks offer excellent camping facilities. Picnic tables are available here as well as in the city park directly behind the field house.

History

As early as 1870, the Uinta Basin was known for its abundant vertebrate fossils. O.C. Marsh from Yale University first identified Eocene (35-45 million years old) mammals in what would later be known as Uintan and Duchesnian age rocks. Subsequently, Earl Douglass of the Carnegie Museum in Pittsburgh, Pennsylvania, who had been researching fossil mammals in the Bonanza area, came to look for dinosaurs. His search of the Jurassic Morrison Formation (145 million years old) near Split Mountain led to the discovery, in 1909, of one of the world's finest concentrations of fossil dinosaur remains. His quarry, 20 miles from Vernal, is now part of Dinosaur National Monument.

Rather than lose the prehistoric wealth of this area to Eastern museums and universities, Arthur G. Nord and others in the community formulated the concept of a field house. In 1945, the Utah Legislature established the Utah Field House of Natural History to house and display "the fossil remains of ancient plant and animal life and other objects of natural history." The field house is now a state park.

Hours

The field house is open daily except Thanksgiving, Christmas, and New Year's Day. Winter hours (Labor Day to Memorial Day) are 9 am to 5 pm. Summer hours are 9 am to 9 pm.

For further information, contact Utah Field House of Natural History State Park, 235 East Main Street, Vernal, UT 84078-2605. ☎ (801) 789-3799.

Utah Lake State Park

Location: 3 miles west of Interstate 15 in Provo.

The park is located at the confluence of the Provo River and Utah Lake for great river and lake-front water play. Sprawling lawns along the shoreline, visitor facilities and a marina support unlimited year-round recreation.

The park is on the east shore of Utah's largest natural freshwater lake. The Cedar Valley Mountains rise abruptly from the lake shore on the west, and the majestic Wasatch Mountains provide panoramic vistas from the north and east.

Special Features

Facilities at Utah Lake State Park include modern restrooms with hot water showers, culinary water sites throughout the park, a sanitary dump station, and an outdoor ice rink. The new sheltered marina has 78 boat docks, courtesy docks, and four cement launching ramps available for both power- and sailboaters. Throughout the park are three group and 35 individual picnic sites with tables and free-standing barbecue grills. The park also has seven acres of maintained lawns.

Activities

Park visitors picnic, camp, and fish. They swim, water-ski, sail, power boat, and ice skate during the winter months. Rollerblading is popular during the summer. Add canoeing and kayaking to round out the list. Others choose to simply sit back and enjoy: sunbathe, throw a frisbee around, play catch, sightsee, or watch birds along the lake's shoreline and wetlands.

Plants & Animals

Except for a few indigenous, long-leaf poplar trees, all other park vegetation has been planted as part of a landscaping program – corkscrew willows, dome willows, weeping willows, hybrid cottonwoods, maples, blue and green spruce, Lombardi poplars, mountain ash, birch and flowering plum.

Wildlife includes pheasants, quail, a variety of shore birds, great horned owls, redtail hawks, Cooper's hawks, skunks, weasels, opossums, raccoons, beavers, and muskrats. Canada geese, mallards, pintails, wood ducks, teals, redheads, canvasbacks, and others like goldeneye and ruddy duck, migrate in and out of the area. An occasional bald or golden eagle can be spotted, as can a great white pelican.

History

Utah Lake State Park was originally called the Provo Boat Harbor. It was donated to the Utah Division of Parks and Recreation in July 1967. Over the next decade, major development projects made the 295-acre park one of Utah's premiere attractions. Unfortunately, flooding in 1982-83 totally destroyed the area, forcing the park to close. Redevelopment efforts during 1985-88 restored it to full operating status.

Today the park and the adjacent 95,900 surface acres of Utah Lake are used by hundreds of thousands of outdoor enthusiasts.

For further information contact Utah Lake State Park, 4400 West Center Street, Provo, UT 84601-9715. ☎ (801) 375-0731.

Veterans Memorial State Park

Location: On SR 68, six miles south of Riverton.

Veterans Memorial State Park serves a dual purpose. First, it is a lasting memorial and burial ground for those who served in the armed forces. Second, the park depicts America's patriotic heritage and beliefs. Located just north of Camp Williams Military Reservation, the park offers a vista of the beautiful Wasatch Mountains.

History

The Utah Military and Veterans Affairs Committee and concerned citizens began work in the early 1970's to establish a Utah veterans cemetery. Land and funding were donated by the state of Utah. Additional money came from the federal government, veterans, citizens, and civic, business and religious communities. Veterans Memorial State Park was dedicated on Memorial Day 1990.

Facilities

The innovative 150-seat chapel, five stories in height, is in the center of the 30-acre park. The chapel is available for funerals and other functions in keeping with the park's theme. A fountain, eternal flame and Wall of Honor are located in the courtyard. The well-manicured grounds are divided by patches of scrub oak.

The administration building houses military artifacts and patriotic items. The Freedom Shrine includes copies of the Constitution, Declaration of Independence, Bill of Rights and other historical documents that relate to the founding of the United States.

Wall of Honor

The Wall of Honor is in the open courtyard between the chapel and administration building. The wall lists names of individuals and organizations who donated $100 or more to the building of the memorial park. This is an ongoing project of the Utah Military and Veterans Affairs Committee.

Interment Policies

The cemetery is available for all veterans of the armed forces, reserves or National Guard who were released under honorable conditions or who died on active duty or during training. Their legal spouses and dependent children also are entitled to burial according to rules of the Department of Veterans Affairs National Cemeteries.

A $100 chapel fee is charged for funerals up to two hours in length. The chapel may be rented for other functions, as determined suitable by the sexton, for the same fee plus a $200 refundable cleaning deposit. Funeral directors will obtain the necessary US flag for veteran burials. Funeral parking is controlled by the funeral director.

Grave sites may not be reserved. A minimum of 24 hours notice is required for burials. They are in a progressive sequence with provisions made for the surviving spouse. Funeral homes must provide a vault for all casket interments.

Only government headstones and markers are allowed. Government headstones are provided and set at no cost for most veterans who served on active duty. Headstones or markers must be privately purchased for veterans not meeting active duty time requirements; usually those who served in the reserves or National Guard only. The sexton will prepare and approve all headstone and marker requests submitted to the Department of Veterans Affairs. Some optional inscriptions are authorized, but at personal expense. Call for costs.

Hours

Veterans Memorial State Park is located at 17111 South Camp Williams Road. The administration building is open weekdays from 9 am to 5 pm. Grounds are open daily from 8 am to 5 pm. No pets or picnicking allowed.

For further information, contact Veterans Memorial State Park, 17111 Camp Williams Road, PO Box 446, Riverton, UT 84065-0446. ☎ (801) 254-9036.

Wasatch Mountain State Park

Location: In the heart of Heber Valley.

Tucked away in Utah's beautiful Wasatch Mountains, Wasatch Mountain State Park is both a summer and winter wonderland. One of Utah's finest 27-hole golf courses is found here. There is camping, picnicking, hiking, and horseback riding. Snowmobiling and cross-country skiing are popular winter activities. The park is just minutes away from the year-round resort, Park City.

Set in beautiful Heber Valley, this is one of Utah's most developed state parks. Park facilities include 139 camping/picnicking areas, two group-use pavilions, modern restrooms, hot showers, and utility hookups. The chalet, a ranch-style building complete with kitchen facilities, is available for summer and winter group outings. Little Deer Creek is an excellent area for group parties and reunions.

For further information contact Wasatch Mountain State Park, PO Box 10, Midway, UT 84049-0010. ☎ (801) 654-1791 (visitor center); (801) 654-0532 (golf course).

Willard Bay State Park

Location: North Marina is 15 miles north of Ogden off I-15;
South Marina is 8 miles north of Ogden.

Willard Bay rests atop the Great Salt Lake flood plain in northern Utah. Its 9,900 acres of fresh water provide boating, waterskiing and year-round fishing for crappie, walleye, and channel catfish. Two state-owned facilities are available to campers.

The north marina is 15 miles north of Ogden, just off Interstate 15. The park has 62 campsites, modern restrooms, hot showers, sewage disposal station, seasonal/transient boat slip rentals, and sandy beaches.

The south marina is eight miles north of Ogden. It is open April through October and provides 30 campsites with modern restrooms.

For further information, contact Willard Bay State Park, 650 North 900 West #A, Willard, UT 84340-9999. ☎ (801) 734-9494.

Yuba State Park

Location: 30 miles south of Nephi, just off Interstate 15.

Yuba Recreation Area, conveniently located in central Utah, offers a host of water recreation opportunities. Warm water, gently sloping beaches and sand dunes attract visitors April through

November. It sits at an elevation of 5,100 feet. The reservoir, when full, is 20 miles long and as much as two miles wide. Yuba Reservoir is the largest of many water impoundments on the Sevier River.

This recreation area is cooperatively managed by the Utah Division of Parks and Recreation and the USDI Bureau of Land Management.

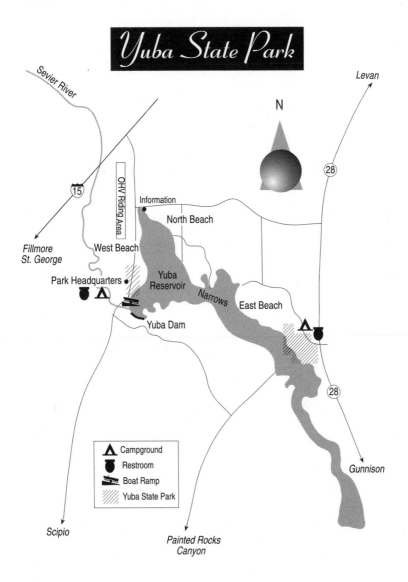

Special Features

Facilities include a 20-unit campground and seven overflow sites, covered group pavilion with picnic tables, group camping area, drinking water, modern restrooms, sewage disposal station, loading docks and boat launching ramp. Handicapped-accessible showers are available for campground patrons. A primitive campground and additional boat launching ramp are located on the east side of the reservoir at Painted Rocks.

The Bureau of Land Management provides primitive camping at North Beach. Facilities include garbage collection points, portable restrooms and ranger station.

Activities

Warm water reaching 70°F during the summer makes the reservoir extremely popular for boating, waterskiing, sailboarding, sailing and swimming. Two boat ramps, one at Yuba State Park and another at Painted Rocks, provide access for all types of watercraft. Year-round fishing is for walleye, perch, catfish, and northern pike. Other activities include camping, picnicking, rockhounding, mountain biking, off-road vehicle expolration in designated areas and waterfowl hunting in season.

History

Long ago, native Americans inhabited the area. Stone tools, broken pottery, rock art and other traces of those cultures are visible today along what used to be the Sevier River. Rock art can be viewed by boat at Painted Rocks just north of the boat ramp. Remnants of prehistoric camps have been discovered in several places around the reservoir. More recent ranching and mining activity also is evident.

Archeologists at the reservoir are attempting to interpret the past through these traces of early life. Feel free to explore. If you discover any artifacts, leave them in place and notify the Utah Division of Parks and Recreation or the Bureau of Land Management.

Fathers Dominquez and Escalante left Santa Fe, New Mexico in July 1776 to find an overland route to Monterey, California. Their well-documented exploration took them through this area in September 1776, where they taught native Americans about Christianity. Modern historic markers depicting the route are at the north end of the reservoir.

Yuba Reservoir, originally named Sevier Bridge Reservoir, was built to store water from the Sevier River for agricultural and industrial uses. Construction on the dam, now called Yuba Dam, started in 1902 and was completed in 1917.

For many years after its construction, the dam was known as U.B. Dam, a name taken from a construction worker's song. It was built by local farmers and ranchers who had the option of doing the hard, tedious labor or losing their water rights. The song lyrics portrayed the workers as damned if they worked and damned if they didn't work. "You be" damned, either way!

For further information, contact Yuba State Park, PO Box 159, Levan, UT 84639-0159. ☎ (801) 758-2611.

National Parks

Arches National Park

Location: 5 miles north of Moab.

The world's largest concentration of natural stone arches is found in Arches National Park. Over 1,500 of these "miracles of nature" grace the 73,000-acre area. A 41-mile paved loop road in the park leads to the major sights, including Balanced Rock, Skyline Arch, Double Arch, and the Fiery Furnace; reservations are required and must be made at the visitor center. The road to the trailhead for famous Delicate Arch is paved, but beyond that, on to the Delicate Arch Viewpoint, it is unpaved but passable to cars.

Arches National Park is open seven days per week, 24 hours each day. The visitor center is open daily, except Christmas, from 8 am to 4:30 pm, and later from mid-April through September. Campfire programs and ranger-guided walks are offered during the summer. Ask about the Junior Ranger program.

Camping

The 52-site Devils Garden Campground is open all year. Individual sites are available on a first-come, first-served basis. You must pre-register at the visitor center or entrance station. A $7 per night fee is charged from March to October, when water is available. Facilities include tables, grills and toilets. Wood gathering in the park is prohibited; bring your own wood or charcoal for the grills. Two group sites are available and may be reserved for 10 or more people. Reservations are taken by mail or telephone beginning January 2nd for the year. The group camping fee is $3 per person per night, with a minimum charge of $30 per night. Children who have not begun first-grade are admitted free. No RVs or campers are permitted in group sites.

Hiking & Exploring

Arches is a great place to explore, but the climate and landscape can cause major problems for the unprepared. Summer temperatures can exceed 100°F (38°C). Carry water (one gallon or four liters per person each day), and wear protective clothing. Winter daytime temperatures are generally comfortable, but at night it often drops below freezing. Plan ahead!

Trails are marked with cairns (piles of rocks). Follow these carefully and stay on the trails. Sandstone "slickrock" is fun to climb on, but can crumble and break easily, and may be slippery. It is much easier to climb up some areas than to get back down. Use your common sense and turn back before you reach your skill limits.

Backcountry permits are available free to charge at the visitor venter. There are no backcountry trails or campsites.

- Stay on the trails so you don't impact the cryptobiotic crust covering the fragile desert soils or the other plant life. **This is very, very important!**
- Be sure to take and drink water. A gallon per person per day is recommended. Don't skimp, even on short trails!
- Wear good hiking or walking shoes.
- Carry out all of your trash, including cigarette butts.
- Leave everything as you found it.

Trails of Arches National Park

All trails are marked on the park brochure map, and are listed here in order as you proceed north into the park from the visitor center.

Delicate Arch: 3 miles, round trip. Fairly non-strenuous trails take visitors to several other arches. There are also backpacking areas and unpaved four-wheel-drive roads.

Desert Nature Trail: 0.2 mile. Start at Arches Visitor Center. A short, self-guided nature walk that follows numbered posts which correspond to a brochure available at the visitor venter.

Park Avenue Trail: 1 mile. Start at South Park Avenue parking area; ending at Courthouse Towers parking area. This easy trail follows a canyon bottom offering a close-up of massive fins and monoliths. Look for potholes after rains. Hikers may begin at one end and be picked up by a driver at the other end. If walking the round trip, it's shorter to retrace your steps on the trail, than to walk along the road (and much more enjoyable!).

Balanced Rock Trail: 0.2 mile. Start at Balanced Rock parking area. A short loop leads to the base of this famous formation. Walk up close to get a real feel for its size!

The Windows: 0.9 mile. Start at Windows parking area. This easy loop leads to North and South Windows and to Ruttet Arch. Return to the parking area along the trail, rather than going "cross-country" through the vegetation and cryptobiotic crust. A slightly longer return via the primitive loop goes around the back of the two Windows, for a view of the Spectacles.

Double Arch Trail: 0.25 mile. Start at Double Arch parking area (just around the loop from the Windows parking area). Take this short, easy stroll and stand under the twin awe-inspiring arches featured in the movie, *Indiana Jones and the Last Crusade.*

Delicate Arch Trail: 1.5 miles (one way). Start at Wolfe Ranch parking area. This moderately strenuous trail crosses a swinging bridge over Salt Wash and continues up the slickrock, finally emerging at the arch. Take water, wear hiking shoes, and avoid the midday heat. There is NO shade along this trail!

Fiery Furnace: Start at Fiery Furnace parking area. Ranger-guided hikes explore this labyrinth of sandstone canyons. Check at the visitor center and the bulletin boards for hike schedules. The moderately strenuous hikes cover about two miles of trail and take 2½ to 3 hours.

No marked trails exist in this area so, unless you are an experienced explorer, join one of the guided hikes. If you do go exploring, be sure to avoid cryptobiotic soils and fragile plant life; walk only on sandstone or in the sandy washes. And don't get lost!

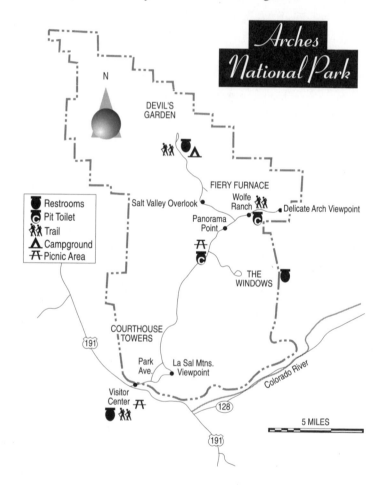

Devil's Garden Trail: 2 miles (round trip) to Landscape Arch, 4 miles (round trip) to Double-O Arch, 5 miles (round trip) to Double-O Arch returning via the primitive loop trail. Start at Devils Garden Trailhead. Longest of the maintained trails in the park, the Devils Garden Trail passes nearly a dozen arches and offers excellent views of the fins, Salt Valley, and the La Sal Mountains. The trail to Landscape Arch is fairly easy, but is somewhat steeper and rockier beyond the arch itself. The primitive trail adds a mile to the return trip and goes down into mysterious Fin Canyon.

Tower Arch Trail: 2 miles, round trip. Start at Tower Arch Trailhead. This moderately strenuous trail leads to a spectacular arch in the Klondike Bluffs area. An alternate, much shorter trail begins at the end of the four-wheel-drive road on the west side of Tower Arch.

Bicycling & Climbing

Bicycles are welcome on roads in the park, but there are no designated bike trails. All bicycles must abide by vehicle regulations and are not allowed on any hiking trails or off established roads.

Technical climbing is permitted, but is only for experienced climbers. Climbing is not allowed on any arches named on the USGS topographic map, nor on Balanced Rock and a few other locations. Check at the visitor center for more information.

Fees

Entrance fees are $4 per vehicle for a seven-day pass into Arches. Individuals walking, on bicycles or motorcycles, or traveling in commercial or charter buses are charged $2 each.

For further information, contact the Superintendent, PO Box 907, Moab, UT 84532, ☎ (801) 259-8161 (voice mail) or (801) 259-5279 (TDD for the hearing impaired).

Bryce Canyon National Park

Location: Take Utah 12 east from US 89. The park entrance is four miles off Route 12 on Utah 63. Utah 12 continues on to Boulder and Capital Reef National Park.

This park is in southwestern Utah within a five-hour drive of 10 other national parks. Following the plateau rim for much of its 18 miles, the park road and its overlooks offer stunning panoramas. To make the most of your visit, stop at the visitor center first. There, you can watch a free slide program, study the exhibits, and browse through books, maps and other publications about the park and surrounding area. The information desk will give you advice on planning your trip.

Thousands of delicately-carved spires rise in brilliant color from the amphitheaters of Bryce Canyon National Park. Millions of years of wind and water at work have etched out the pink cliffs of the canyon. The most brilliant hues come alive with the rising and setting of the sun.

Bryce Canyon offers more than driving tours. Rangers conduct walks, talks, and campfire programs in summer, on topics ranging from geology and wildlife to air quality. Some 50 miles of hiking trails offer prospects of close encounters with hoodoos. A number of trails lead down among them from overlooks on the main park road. Just a short walk will leave you surrounded by these unusual rock formations. Horseback rides are also popular here.

Driving Along the Plateau Rim

A scenic drive along the 18 miles of the main park road affords outstanding views of the park and southern Utah scenery. From many overlooks you can see over 100 miles on clear days. On crisp winter days, views from Rainbow or Yovimpa points are restricted only by the curvature of the Earth. Driving south from the visitor center to Rainbow Point, you gradually gain 1,100 feet of elevation. En route, watch how the forests change from ponderosa pine to spruce, fir and aspen. Trailers are not permitted beyond Sunset Campground. You may park them at the visitor center or Sunset Point parking lot. All overlooks lie east of the road. To avoid crossing traffic to reach them, drive to the southern end of the park and stop at the overlooks on your return.

Hoodoos Cast Their Spell

Hoodoo – a pillar of rock, usually of fantastic shape, left by erosion.

Hoodoo – to cast a spell.

At Bryce Canyon National Park erosion forms a remarkable array of fantastic shapes we know as hoodoos. Surrounded by the beauty of southern Utah, these hoodoos cast their spell on all who visit. Geologists say that 10 million years ago forces within the Earth created and then moved the massive blocks we know as the Squarius and Paunsaugunt plateaus. Rock layers on the Squarius now tower 2,000 feet above the same layers on the Paunsaugunt. Ancient rivers carved the tops and exposed edges of these blocks, removing some layers and sculpting intricate formations in others. The Paria Valley was created and later widened between the plateaus.

The Paria River and its many tributaries continue to carve the plateau edges. Rushing waters carry dirt and gravel between the gully edges and steep slopes of the Paunsaugunt Plateau on which Bryce Canyon National Park lies. With time, tall thin ridges called fins emerge. Fins further erode into pinnacles and spires called hoodoos. These in turn weaken and fall, adding their bright colors to the hills below.

History

Early native Americans left little to tell us of their lives in the plateaus. We know that people have been in the Colorado Plateau region for about 12,000 years, but only random fragments of worked stone tell of their presence near Bryce Canyon. Artifacts give a more detailed story at lower elevations beyond the park's boundary. Both Anasazi and Fremont influences are found near the park. The people of each culture left bits of a puzzle to be pieced together by present and future archeologists.

Paiutes lived in the region when Euro-Americans arrived in southern Utah. Paiutes explained the colorful hoodoos as "Legend People" who were turned to stone by Coyote. The Paiutes were living throughout the area when Capt. Clarence E. Dutton explored here with John Wesley Powell in the 1870s. Many of today's place names come from this time. Dutton's report gave the name Pink Cliffs to the Claron Formation. Other names – Paunsaugunt, place or home of the beavers; Paria, muddy water or elk water; Panguitch, water or fish; and Yovimpa, point of pines – were derived from the Paiute language.

The Paiutes were displaced by emissaries of the LDS Church who developed the many small communities throughout Utah. Ebenezer Bryce aided in the settlement of southwestern Utah and northern Arizona. In 1875 he came to the Paria Valley to live and harvest timber from the plateau. Neighbors called the canyon behind his home Bryce's Canyon. Today it remains the name not only of one canyon, but also of a national park.

Shortly after 1900, visitors were coming to see the colorful geologic sights, and the first accommodations were built along the Paunsaugunt Plateau rim above Bryce's Canyon. By 1920 efforts were started to set aside these scenic wonders. In 1923 President Warren G. Harding proclaimed part of the Bryce Canyon National Monument under the Powell (now Dixie) National Forest. In 1924 legislation was passed to establish the area as a Utah national park, but the provisions of this legislation were not met until 1928. Legislation was passed that year to change the name of the new park to Bryce Canyon National Park.

Each year the park is visited by more than 1.5 million tourists from all over the world. Languages as varied as the shapes and colors of the hoodoos express pleasure in the sights. Open all year, the park offers recreational opportunities in each season. Hiking, sightseeing, and photography are the most popular summer activities. Spring and fall months offer greater solitude. In the winter months, quiet combines with the area's best air quality for unparalleled views and serenity beyond compare. In all seasons, fantastic shapes cast their spell to remind us of what we protect here in Bryce Canyon National Park.

Accessibility: The paved, fairly level trail between Sunset and Sunrise points and many viewpoints, park buildings, and restrooms are accessible to people in wheelchairs. Handicapped-accessible campsites are available. The visitor center slide program is captioned.

Weather: From April through October, days are pleasant and nights cool. Thunderstorms are common in summer. Winter features many bright and crisp days with snow blanketing the plateau like icing on a cake. Many park viewpoints remain open in winter, and lodging is available year-round near the park. Snowshoeing and cross-country skiing are popular winter activities.

Facilities

Camping: Tent and RV camping is available on a first-come, first-served basis at North and Sunset campgrounds. A fee is charged; length of stay is limited to 14 days per visit, 30 days per year. Sites have picnic tables and fireplaces; water and restrooms are nearby.

One group site is available by advance reservation only. Buy or bring firewood; wood gathering is prohibited. There are no hook-ups. A complimentary sanitary dump station is provided near North Campground in summer.

Church Services: Non-denominational and LDS services are held in the park on summer Sundays. Other services are offered in neighboring communities.

Walking & Hiking

Perhaps the best way to experience both the grandeur and intimacy of Bryce's forests, meadows, and startling erosional features is on foot. Maps and information are available at the visitor center (and nature center during summer months). Carry drinking water, wear sturdy footgear, and remember that your return will be uphill. Overnight backcountry excursions require a free permit available at the nature center (or visitor center). These trips are allowed only on the Under-the-Rim and Riggs Spring trails.

Wildlife

Bryce Canyon's forests and meadows support diverse animal life, from small mammals and birds to foxes and occasional mountain lions and black bears. Keep a healthy distance from wildlife; feeding or approaching causes problems for the animals and can be dangerous to you. Do not disturb their eating behavior and natural wariness.

For further information, contact Superintendent, Bryce Canyon National Park, Bryce Canyon, UT 84717. ☎ (801) 834-5322.

Capitol Reef National Park

Location: The visitor center is 11 miles (19 km) east of Torrey on UT 24.

Capitol Reef National Park splashes vibrant color for 75 miles from its northern to southern boundaries. Most of Capitol Reef is an inviting wilderness of sandstone formations and cliffs, such as Capitol Dome, Hickman Bridge, the Waterpocket Fold and splendid Cathedral Valley. In the midst of Capitol Reef's red rocks are large orchards, where fruit may be picked in season, and the remnants of Fruita, an early pioneer settlement. The visitor center is open year-round. Several fairly easy hiking trails and the 25-mile Scenic Drive lead from the vicinity of the visitor center. Cathedral Valley and other areas may be reached via high-clearance dirt roads.

Camping

Fruita Campground: 63 RV sites, seven tent sites, picnic tables, toilets, dump site, fee charged, handicapped facilities, group site. Open year-round.

Capitol Reef Trails

All distances are ONE-WAY, except for those marked with an asterisk (*), which are loop trails.

Very Easy - smooth path over level ground.
Easy - uneven ground, but fairly level.
Moderate - some steep grades, some level sections of trail.
Strenuous - steep grades, uneven terrain and long, steady climbs.

NOTE: Be sure to carry water with you, even on the short hikes. Most water in Capitol Reef is contaminated with mineral or by animals.

Capitol Gorge: 1 mile. Easy; mostly level walking along narrow wash bottom with sheer canyon walls plus Pioneer Register and waterpockets or "tanks."

Cassidy Arch: 1¾ miles. Strenuous; climbs steeply from floor of Grand Wash to high cliffs, ending above the arch.

Capitol Reef National Park

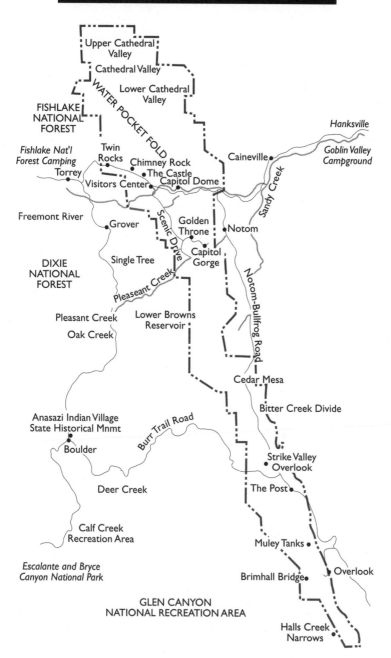

Upper Cathedral Valley

Cathedral Valley

Lower Cathedral Valley

WATER POCKET FOLD

FISHLAKE NATIONAL FOREST

Hanksville

Fishlake Nat'l Forest Camping

Twin Rocks

Chimney Rock

Caineville

Goblin Valley Campground

Torrey

The Castle

Visitors Center

Capitol Dome

Sandy Creek

Freemont River

Grover

Scenic Drive

Golden Throne

Notom

Single Tree

Capitol Gorge

DIXIE NATIONAL FOREST

Pleaseant Creek

Notom-Bullfrog Road

Pleasant Creek

Lower Browns Reservoir

Oak Creek

Cedar Mesa

Bitter Creek Divide

Anasazi Indian Village State Historical Mnmt

Burr Trail Road

Boulder

Strike Valley Overlook

Deer Creek

The Post

Calf Creek Recreation Area

Muley Tanks

Escalante and Bryce Canyon National Park

Overlook

Brimhall Bridge

GLEN CANYON NATIONAL RECREATION AREA

Halls Creek Narrows

Chimney Rock: 3½* miles. Strenuous; climbs up switchbacks to upper loop; views of Chimney Rock and panoramas; self-guiding nature trail.

Cohab Canyon: 1¾ miles. Strenuous for first quarter-mile, then moderate; climbs to a hidden canyon above the campground.

Fremont Gorge Overlook: 2¼ miles. Strenuous; crosses Johnson Meas, then climbs steeply to 1,000 feet above Fremont River; self-guiding nature trail.

Fremont River: 1¼ miles. Very easy first half-mile, strenuous thereafter; through orchards to overlook of the valley.

Frying Pan: 3 miles. Strenuous; follows ridge of Capitol Reef escarpment.

Golden Throne: 2 miles. Strenuous; climbs from bottom of gorge to top of cliffs, ending near the base of Golden Throne; panoramas.

Goosenecks: One-tenth of a mile. Easy; views of Sulphur Creek Canyon, panoramas, interesting rock formations beside the trail.

Grand Wash: 2¼ miles. Easy; mostly level walking along narrow wash bottom with sheer canyon walls on both sides.

Hickman Bridge: 1 mile. Moderate; self-guiding nature trail leads under Hickman Natural Bridge.

Navajo Knobs: 4½ miles. Strenuous; follows trail to Rim Overlook; then climbs another 2¼ miles for a 350-degree panorama.

Old Wagon Trail: 3½* miles. Strenuous; follows wagon route on Miners Mountain; panoramic views of the Waterpocket Fold.

Rim Overlook: 2¼ miles. Strenuous; ends on top of 1,000-foot cliffs with spectacular views of the orchards, campgrounds and southward along the Waterpocked Fold.

Sunset Point: Third of a mile. Easy; panoramic views of cliffs and domes; dramatic lighting at day's end.

For further information, contact the Superintendent, Capitol Reef National Park, Torrey, Utah 84775. ☎ (801) 425-3791.

Zion National Park

*Location: Two entrances to Zion Canyon are 33 miles
east of I-15 or 12 miles west of US 89, both on State Route 9.
The Kolob Canyons section of the park is accessible off I-15.*

Zion is part of the Southwest's "Grand Circle" of national parks, monuments, historical areas, and recreation areas – one of the world's great concentrations of outstanding natural and cultural features. Even though these areas may seem close, do not try to visit too many in a short period.

One of the nation's oldest national parks, Zion has a quiet grandeur that is unique. The six-mile drive into the heart of Zion Canyon brings visitors past such scenic wonders as The Great White Throne, The Watchman, Grotto Picnic Area, Angels Landing, Weeping Rock, the trail to Emerald Pools and the fantastic Gateway to the Narrows Trail, which is suitable for strollers and wheelchairs with assistance. After millions of years, the Virgin River continues to flow through the masterpiece it has created.

Zion is a spot where the word scenic does not do justice. It is a backpackers paradise, yet the park can be equally enjoyed from a motorized tram. Other popular ways to see the canyon are on horseback with one of the outfitters in the park, by bicycle, or on the guided walks and evening programs offered during the summer.

Kolob Canyons

Kolob Canyons, the northwestern section of Zion National Park, features spectacular narrow canyons and brightly-colored, towering vertical cliffs. Excellent views of the canyons are possible along the five-mile scenic drive. A picnic area is located at the end of the drive.

Cedar Breaks National Monument

Cedar Breaks National Monument, in the high country north of Zion, is a mixture of alpine and canyon country splendors. A multicolored limestone amphitheater, with spires, hoodoos and etched ridgelines is the primary feature. The amphitheater is rimmed by cool forests and colorful alpine meadows.

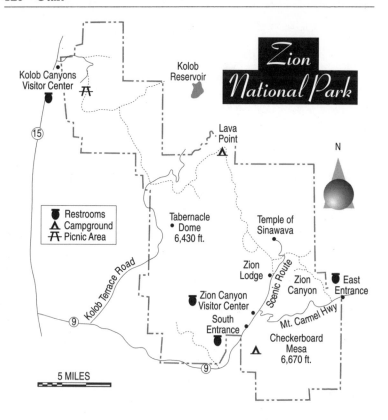

Pipe Spring National Monument

Pipe Spring National Monument is a little-known gem of the park system rich with American Indian, early explorer and western pioneer history. A fort, built in the 1870's by Mormon pioneers, laid claim to one of the few natural springs in the area. The fort, several ranch buildings, living history demonstrations, and an interpretive trail offer a glimpse of American Indian and pioneer life in the Old West.

Backpacking

Free permits are required for all backcountry camping. Group size is limited to 12 persons for both day use and overnight trips. Permits and hiking information are available at the visitor center.

Bicycling

Bicycles are permitted only on established roads and the Pa'rus Trail. The Pa'rus Trail leads from the campgrounds to the Scenic Drive junction. Riding on hiking trails or cross-country is prohibited.

Riding bicycles through the Zion-Mt. Carmel Tunnel is not allowed. Bicycles must be transported through the tunnel by a motor vehicle.

Horseback Riding

At Zion Lodge, guided trips are available March through October. Reservations are advised. ☎ (801) 772-3967.

Climbing

Many of Zion's sandstone cliffs are comprised of loose or "rotten rocks." Climbing hardware and techniques that may be appropriate for granite are often less effective on sandstone. Information on climbing is available at the visitor center. A permit is required for overnight climbs.

Trails of Zion National Park

Weeping Rock Trail: 0.8 mile. Start at Zion Canyon Scenic Drive/Weeping Rock parking lot. This easy, paved trail ends at a rock alcove with dripping springs. Hanging gardens and wildflowers decorate the walls in spring and summer.

Riverside Walk: 2-3 miles. Start at the Temple of Sinawava. Another paved trail which, despite minor drop-offs, is an easy stroll. It offers trailside exhibits, wildflowers and hanging gardens.

Lower Emerald Pools Trail: 1.5 miles. Start opposite the Zion Lodge. This handicapped-accessible trail takes you to a pool and three waterfalls.

Middle Pool Trail: 2 miles. Start opposite the Zion Lodge. A moderate trail with long drop-offs and loops leading to the lower and middle pools.

Canyon Overlook Trail: 1-1.5 miles. Start long the Zion-Mt. Carmel Hwy., just east of Long Tunnel. Despite being rocky and uneven, this trail is relatively easy. It ends at a spectacular viewpoint over Lower Zion Canyon and Pine Creek Canyon.

Wathchman Trail: 2-3.3 miles. Start at the service road of Watchman Campground registration station. This moderate trail is best attempted in early or late day due to the heat. The overlook at the end of the trail shows Lower Zion Canyon, Oak Creek Canyon and the town of Springdale.

Hidden Canyon Trail: 2-3 miles. Another moderate trail, Hidden Canyon leads through a narrow side canyon and should not be undertaken by those fearful of heights. The trail ends at the mouth of the canyon, although you can hike an extra half-mile to a natural arch.

Angels Landing Trail: 5-8 miles. This is classified as a strenuous excursion and, as with the Hidden Canyon Trail, should not be attempted by anyone with a fear of heights. The last half-mile of the trail follows a steep, narrow ridge where chains have been added to help hikers make their way to the lofty summit.

Observation Point Trail: 8-12 miles. Start at the Weeping Rock parking lot. A six-hour, strenuous hike through Echo Canyon to Observation Point.

West Rim Trail: 10-17 miles. A strenuous climb to a high-country viewpoint of canyons and an isolated mesa. The trail continues to Lava Point, an alternate starting point. The latter section should not be attempted as part of a day hike.

Camping

In the park: Watchman and South campgrounds are near the south entrance of the park.

Individual campsites are available on a first-come, first-served basis. Arrival before noon generally ensures a site. The fee is $8 nightly or $4 for holders of Golden Age/Access cards.

Lava Point is a six-site primitive campground with no water and no fee. Open June through November.

Outside the park: Private campgrounds (with showers and hook-ups) are available in Springdale and adjacent to the east entrance of the park.

Weather Conditions

Summer temperatures can exceed 110°F. Carry and drink plenty of water, even if you do not feel thirsty. Thirst is the first symptom of dehydration!

This is flash flood country. Stay out of the rivers, narrow canyons, and washes, when it is raining or threatening to rain. Be alert for lightning, especially in open areas and on the high rim trails. Unexpected storms can develop quickly!

Due to the growing number of visitors to Zion and the limited road system, over-sized vehicles entering the park's east or south entrances will be subject to special restrictions and a $10 charge for escort service through the narrow Long Tunnel.

Note: On April 12, 1995, a naturally occurring landslide briefly dammed the Virgin River. In its efforts to find a new course, the river washed out about 200 yards of the Scenic Drive. The Zion Canyon Scenic Drive was temporarily closed while repairs were made. Always check for current conditions. Rangers will be more than happy to help you find alternative routes.

New Mexico

State Parks

The size and terrain of New Mexico's lake parks vary from small, heavily wooded mountain lakes to vast warm-water reservoirs. The opportunity for water sports is endless – stream and lake fishing, jet boating and waterskiing, sailing and wind surfing, swimming and scuba diving.

The state's northern parks include some of the most beautiful scenery in the western United States. Set within high mountain ranges is a land of hidden lakes, quiet streams and rushing rivers. Cool green forests and meadows brimming with wildflowers call hikers, campers and photographers to behold an unheard of beauty.

Warm desert days draw snow-weary Northerners (snowbirds) to the desert parks each winter. The Chihuahuan Desert lowlands and mountains include some of the state's most unique geological formations and natural oddieites. A "city of rocks" aburptly rises out of the plains, lush springs seep from craggy canyon walls and cactus gardens bloom in vivid colors. Few wonders of the world compare in beauty.

Camping & Hiking

Most of New Mexico's parks, national monuments, rivers and forests are dotted with campsites and laced with trails. On the road, you can usually find a commercial RV hook-up complete with cable TV.

Be sure to get your campsite early, especially during the summer and fall months. Sites are available for a small fee on a first-come, first-served basis. Developed campsites usually include running water, restrooms, and even RV hookups. You do not need a permit for camping and hiking in a national forest wilderness area, but they are required in national parks and monuments.

On the trail be sure to take along plenty of warm gear and do not count on finding water along the way. Check with the governing agency to see whether fires are permitted in the area you are planning to visit. And do not go without a good map. Fairly good backcountry maps are available from most government agencies, including the BLM (Bureau of Land Management) and the various Forest Service district headquarters. For more tips on hiking, see section at the beginning of this book.

Annual entrance and camping permits may be purchased at any state park or at the New Mexico State Park division office in Santa Fe.

Hunting & Fishing

Hunting and fishing is limited to designated areas and in accordance with New Mexico Game and Fish regulations and licensing requirements.

Big game such as deer, elk, bears and sheep abound in the mountains, while on the plains you can stalk everything from antelope to ibex and oryx. Small game ranges from squirrels and rabbits to turkeys and waterfowl. For fishermen, New Mexico's lakes are filled with finned denizens, including bass, perch, catfish, walleye, Kokanee salmon and five species of trout.

For licenses and regulations, write:

New Mexico Department of Game and Fish
PO Box 25112
Santa Fe, New Mexico 87504
(505) 827-7911

If you call ☎ 800-ASK-FISH you will get an informative recorded message detailing licenses, regulations, fishing hotspots and current conditions.

Horseback Riding

Horseback riding is permitted only in designated areas at certain parks. Riders should check with the park for regulations and restrictions prior to arrival.

Boating

Despite its reputation for dryness, New Mexico's numerous lakes and reservoirs make the entire state a boating paradise. Paddlers, fishermen, pleasure cruisers and water skiers will find water and boat ramps at more than 45 state parks, dams, and other lakes.

Remember, swim at your own risk. Swimming is not permitted within 150 feet of a boat ramp, dock, marina, or dam. Skin or scuba diving may be prohibited in certain areas.

Waterskiing is also prohibited within 150 feet of any dock, ramp, mooring area, boat, angler or swimmer. A fluorescent orange or red warning flag at least 12" by 12" must be raised and visible when a skier is starting, stopping or has fallen. All skiers must wear a flotation device. Using a vessel to tow a person engaged in an activity such as waterskiing is prohibited from one hour after sunset until one hour before sunrise.

Northern New Mexico offers some of the best whitewater thrills and chills in the country. Every spring and summer, rafters and kayakers congregate on the banks of the Chama River and upper Rio Grande to ride the swift currents, while others take to quieter but still fast-moving waters for float trips. The water level is best from late May through late July, but some stretches along the Rio Grande are negotiable all year.

Birding

Owing to its wide variety of habitats and its location along the Central Flyway (a major feeding and resting area in the center of New Mexico), this is prime birding country. From dry desert to marshy bog to thick alpine forest, each habitat hosts its share of colorful feathered friends. Finches, swallows and bluebirds glide through high-desert greenery. Quail, doves, and road-runners are seen in the prairie grasses. At the Bosque del Apache Wildlife Refuge near Socorro, thousands of birds – including the whooping crane and bald eagle – stop over during winter and spring migrations. For more information, contact the state office of the National Audubon Society:

> National Audubon Society
> PO Box 9314
> Santa Fe, NM 87504

Rockhounding

Rockhounds will be happy to know that there are places in New Mexico where you can legally collect and cart away stones of all kinds, from agates and opals to turquoise and jasper. The most popular of these spots is Rock Hound State Park, 14 miles east of Deming. This park is completely dedicated to the sport of leaving no stone unturned. You can pitch a tent and spend all the time you want hunting rocks.

The Bureau of Mines and Mineral Resources in Socorro will provide you with a guide to rockhounding locations as well as information on the Rock Hound Roundup in mid-March, where more than 500 rockhounders from 40 different states gather for guided rock trips, auctions and judging.

A Few Tips....

The high altitude increases the potency of the sun's rays. Visitors should always take a hat and sunscreen for outside activities.

Climate. The region's climate makes dehydration a danger for outdoor enthusiasts. Summertime hikers and backpackers should carry about one gallon of water per person each day.

Winter travelers should also remember that snow and subzero temperatures are common here. Warm winter clothes are a must from October through March, and accessories such as tire chains are also recommended.

Time Zones. New Mexico and the Navajo Reservations observe Mountain Daylight Time from April through October. Arizona and the Hopi Reservation, however, remain on Mountain Standard Time year-round. Travelers should consult maps and call ahead to avoid confusion.

Want to Know More?

New Mexico Dept. of Tourism
PO Box 20003
Santa Fe, NM 84503
(505) 801-5400

New Mexico State Parks
408 Galisteo; PO Box 1147
Santa Fe, NM 87504
(505) 827-7456;
in NM 800-451-2541

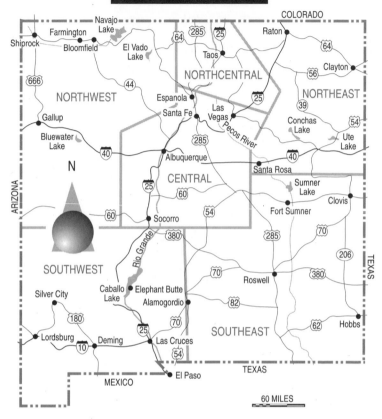

Northwest New Mexico

Bluewater Lake - A Desert Treasure

Location: Take exit #63 off of I-40, then take NM 412 to the lake.

If boating and fishing are your pleasures, take a side trip to Bluewater Lake, one of the true jewels of the New Mexico desert.

Now a state park, the area is inhabited by year-round residents as well as those with summer cabins.

Summer weekends are the busiest time at the lake. Campers, picnickers, and boaters use it from late Friday afternoon until sundown on Sunday. The middle of the week is the best time to find a good camping spot, but the festive air on the weekend is also an attraction and just might be worth the wait for a campsite. Pack a picnic lunch or stop for fast food on the way, but be prepared to want to return to this idyllic spot.

For more information, ☎ (505) 876-4010.

El Vado Lake State Park

Location: From US 84 at Tierra Amarilla,
El Vado is 14 miles southwest on SR 112

ocated in New Mexico's northern mountains, this 1,730-acre state park offers 67 camping sites that are open year-round. The lake covers 3,380 acres at full pool, but averages only 550 acres. Hiking and backpacking are popular activities. There is the trailhead near the entrance that leads to a five-mile trail along the canyon of the Rio Chama to the dam at Heron Lake. Below the dam is a more challenging trail extending through the Rio Chama Canyon to Abiquiu Reservoir.

The Rio Chama can be floated above and below El Vado for those who favor rafting. Downstream is a 33-mile whitewater trip to Abiquiu Reservoir.

For further information contact the Park Superintendent, El Vado Lake State Park, ☎ (505) 588-7247.

Heron Lake State Park

Location: From US 84 at Tierra Amarilla, 11 miles west on SR 95.

picturesque lake set among tall pines, Heron has been designated a "quiet lake" where boats operate at no-wake speeds only.

The park is known for its excellent sailing, fishing, cross-country skiing and hiking.

The canyon of the Rio Chama below the dam is scenic. A spur road east of the dam leads to a trail, which follows the canyon through the Rio Chama Wildlife and Fishing Area to El Vado Lake (see above). This 4,100-acre state park also offers 60 campsites.

Hiking opportunities are limited to the Rio Chama Trail, 5½ miles to El Vado Lake. Fishermen will be drawn by trout and kokanee salmon. Rafters will be challenged by the Rio Chama.

For further information contact the Park Superintendent, ☎ (505) 588-7470.

Navajo Lake State Park

Location: 25 miles east of Bloomfield via US 64 and NM 511.

Navajo is one of New Mexico's largest state parks. The elevation is 6,100 feet.

Camping fees in the park are $7 for a site with no hookups; $11 for a site with electricity; and $13 per night with a full hookup. No reservations are accepted. The park operates on a first-come, first-served basis.

Navajo Dam & Lake

Navajo Dam, a separate park within the state park, is almost three-quarters of a mile long and 400 feet high. This earth- and rock-filled embankment contains three "zones" of selected cobbles, gravel, sand and clay.

The spillway, 138 feet wide in the main section, has a capacity of 34,000 cubic feet per second (254,320 gallons per second). Under normal conditions, water is released into the San Juan River downstream through the outlet works. Water from the river is used for irrigation, municipal and industrial purposes, by oil and gas fields and by thermal powerplants along the San Juan River below the dam to the Shiprock, New Mexico area.

The lake is 35 miles long and has over 150 miles of rugged shore-line. It is fed by the melting snowpack from the surrounding mountains and hills. When filled, the lake covers 15,610 acres. Its blue-green waters lap against shores seldom invaded by man.

Navajo Lake is the principal storage reservoir for the extensive Navajo Indian Irrigation Project. This project is designed to irrigate about 110,000 acres of land on the Navajo Indian Reservation. Just upstream from the dam, on the south, is an intake structure for a tunnel that carries water to these lands.

Construction of the Navajo Indian Irrigation Project was started in 1963, and the first project water was delivered in 1976. Currently, several tunnels, siphons and canals are in operation.

This all-Indian project was designed and is still being constructed by the Bureau of Reclamation for the Bureau of Indian Affairs. Reclamation's Upper Colorado Region, located in Salt Lake City, Utah, is responsible for construction management. As the blocks are completed, they are turned over to the Navajo Tribe for operation and maintenance.

Damsite investigations were made in this vicinity as early as 1904, but the first proposal for a major San Juan River dam was made in 1930. High estimated construction costs delayed authorization until the dam could be incorporated into the revenue-sharing features of the Colorado River Storage Project.

Construction of Navajo Dam began in July 1958. The earth and rock needed for building were taken from 16 borrow areas beside the San Juan River and along benches overlooking the valley. All private land was purchased, and about 50 families moved to other locations. In the reservoir area, the small village of Rosa, New Mexico, was inundated.

Navajo Dam was dedicated September 15, 1962.

Colorado River Storage Project (CRSP)

The CRSP is a basin-wide project for development and use of the water resources of the Upper Colorado River. It is one of the most complex and extensive river-water resource developments in the world. It takes in the drainage area of the Upper Colorado River Basin, encompassing parts of Wyoming, Utah, Colorado, Arizona and New Mexico, about one-twelfth of the area of the continental United States. CRSP dams and reservoirs at Glen Canyon, Flaming Gorge, Navajo and Blue Mesa stabilize the erratic flows of the Colorado River and its main tributaries. This ensures that water commitments to the Lower Basin States – California, Arizona and Nevada – can be met even in years of minimal precipitation. The water remaining in the Upper Basin serves the needs of farmers, municipalities and industries.

Revenues from hydropower generation help repay costs of constructing the widespread CRSP facilities. Eventually, 83% of the construction costs will be repaid to the Federal Treasury.

History

Ancient spearpoints and other artifacts indicate man has lived in the land of the San Juan and Pine rivers for thousands of years. Remains of surface and cave dwellings represent the earliest known villages of the Southwest.

Bits of pottery and the ruins of shallow pit-houses indicate a settled life of farming existed as early as 400 to 700 A.D. During that period, simple pottery was developed and surface dwellings and storage rooms were built with upright poles daubed with mud. Improved methods of farming, masonry construction and more ornamental and refined pottery had been developed by 950 A.D. Around 1050 A.D., the area was apparently abandoned, probably due to drought and erosion of the agricultural fields.

The Navajo Lake area is believed to have remained unpopulated until the 14th century, when vanguards of the Ute and Navajo tribes moved in from the north. These tribes shared dominion over much of the area until the late 1880's. Remnants of their pottery and their forked-stick hogans called "pueblitos" – small masonry dwellings constructed in defensive locations for protection against raids by other tribes – are found throughout the area.

Spanish and Mexican traders and explorers penetrated the region in the 1760's. The famous Dominguez-Escalante Expedition rode through the Arboles, Colorado area in 1776, searching for a route from Santa Fe, New Mexico, to Monterey, California. From 1830 to 1848, traders herded horses by the hundreds over the Old Spanish Trail, which also passed near Arboles.

By 1870, settlers were moving in, pressuring the Indians to live on reservations and opening the way for a rapid influx of prospectors, farmers and stockmen. The Denver and Rio Grande Western Railroad pushed its tracks through the area in the early 1880's.

Although the land was found to be generally arid, agriculture was possible with irrigation. Private canal projects and, later, Federal Reclamation projects, have done much to boost the agricultural possibilities of the region.

Rock formations surrounding Navajo Lake are sedimentary sandstones and shales deposited about 50 million years ago. They are part of the San José Formation of the Eocene age. Occasional fossils of bones and trees are found in this type of formation. A few million years ago, as it carved its canyons, the ancestral San Juan River left high gravel terraces on hilltops.

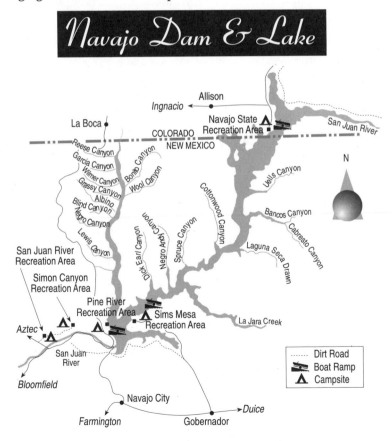

Plants & Animals

Several species of cactus and the bayonet-tipped yucca grow throughout the area. Cottonwoods, willows, tamarisks, Utah junipers and pinons are found at the lake's edge. Ponderosa pine grows at higher elevations.

Several species of fish inhabit the lake, including rainbow and brown trout, fokanee salmon, and channel catfish, crappie, northern pike and large- and smallmouth bass. Below the dam, the San Juan River (New Mexico's largest river) is the home of good-size rainbow, brown and cutthroat trout. It is a designated "Quality Water Fishing Area" with a limit of one trout (20" or longer) per person. It also has a quarter-mile stretch that is catch and release only – no fish may be kept. Only flies and lures with single barbless hooks may be used in the entire 3½-mile-long Quality Water area. Shoreside, you will find numerous deer, elk, rabbits and an occasional raccoon. A quiet, careful observer can also see foxes, coyotes or bobcats. Lizards are common during the warm summer months and a variety of snakes live in the rocky and brushy areas. Rattlesnakes are rarely seen.

Wild animals abound in the nearby hills, and trout and bass flourish in the lake.

Facilities

For those who like boating, marinas, docks and launching ramps are available in both New Mexico and Colorado. Once away from developed areas, boaters may camp or picnic where they choose in New Mexico; Colorado allows camping in designated areas only. All types of boats are allowed on Navajo Lake as long as they meet Coast Guard safety requirements.

The marinas offer boat rentals. For more information, ☎ (505) 632-3245 for the Pine River Marina or (505) 320-0885 for the Sims Mesa Marina.

Land-based explorers will find areas to enjoy, too. The more developed sites include shaded campgrounds and picnic areas. An escape into the wilderness can be made from one of the many semi-developed and primitive roads leading down to the lake.

Visitors are encouraged to make local inquiries about the current conditions of these roads.

Pine Site is the most developed of the three camping areas. It has showers, full hookups, boat ramp and a full-service marina. It is a half-mile north of the dam on NM Highway 511. It also has a small visitor center with extensive, interpretive displays. A 5,000-foot paved airstrip is close by. **Sims Mesa**, like Pine, is set on the lake. It is a more remote area, but it does have modern restrooms, electrical hookups, a boat ramp, and a full -service marina. Dry boat storage is offered here. Its access is via a paved road off US Highway 64, about 25 miles east of the dam. The **San Juan River Site**, nestled in a large cottonwood grove about five miles below the dam, straddles the San Juan River. It features a beautiful campground with modern handicap-accessible facilities. There are picnic areas and access parking areas for anglers. Access is a quarter-mile west of the Aztec bridge on NM 173.

Navajo State Recreation Area in Colorado has a boat ramp, docks, marina, restaurant, general store, and dry boat storage. Rental boats and gasoline are available at the marina. The area also has a visitor center with interpretive displays, modern campgrounds and picnic areas, a nature trail, and a 3,100-foot improved dirt airstrip.

Fishing

Navajo Lake contains both cold- and warm-water species of game fish. The lake's cold-water population – brown and rainbow trout and kokanee salmon – are found at greater depths during the warm summer months and can be caught using a variety of methods. During their autumn spawning run, kokanee salmon may be legally snagged since they die soon afterward. Largemouth bass, crappie, bluegill and channel catfish can be found in warmer waters.

Millions of rainbow trout, salmon and largemouth bass have been stocked in the lake since completion of Navajo Dam.

Before Navajo Dam was completed, the San Juan River was often muddy and filled with silt. With the exception of channel catfish, game fish were almost nonexistent in the river. Now the water below the dam runs cold and clear – an ideal habitat for brown, rainbow and cutthroat trout. A 3¾-mile stretch of the San Juan

River below the dam has been designated "quality fishing water," with special angling regulations.

State fishing licenses are required in both New Mexico and Colorado. Inquire at the marinas or at the visitor centers for complete details.

Hunting

The pinon-covered hills around Navajo Lake offer deer and elk hunting. Management techniques such as reseeding with grasses and browse plants make the area even more attractive to these animals.

Waterfowl are naturally drawn to a large body of water such as Navajo Lake. Large flocks of ducks gather in some parts of the lake, especially in the fall, but the best duck hunting can usually be found in the marshy areas along the San Juan River below the dam.

Hunters must obtain state licenses and observe all regulations and restrictions.

For further information contact the Park Superintendent, ☎ (505) 632-2278.

Red Rock State Park

Location: 6 miles east of downtown Gallup via I-40.

This park, owned and operated by the city of Gallup, includes its own rodeo arena and museum.

The spectacular red cliffs which frame the park on three sides began forming 205 million years ago, during the Mesozoic era, sometimes referred to as the Age of the Dinosaurs. Several archeological sites in the park record the presence of the Anasazi, a prehistoric farming culture which developed and persisted in the area from 300 to 1200 A.D. From 1700 to the present, the region has been sparsely inhabited by the Navajo Indians.

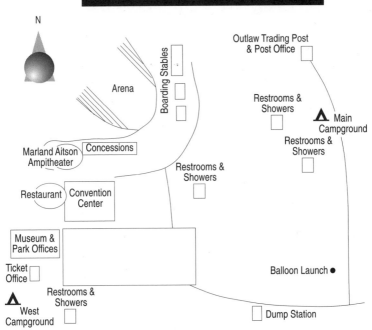

Plants & Animals

Skunks, ground squirrels, prairie dogs and cottontails may be seen in the southwestern region. Other less-common mammals include the bobcat, coyote, and red fox. Lizards and the harmless gopher snake are prevalent in the park. Rattlesnakes are rarely seen, but be aware, they sometimes inhabit the range. The pinon jay, bluebird, raven robin, house sparrow, starling, red-shafted flicker, rock wren, sparrow hawk, red-tailed hawk and mourning dove may be seen throughout New Mexico. Grama grass, Indian rice grass, rabbit-brush, and saltbush grow among the pinon pine and juniper trees.

Inter-Tribal Indian Ceremonial

Red Rock State Park hosts the world famous Inter-Tribal Indian Ceremonial held the second weekend in August. Among the festivities are the colorful Indian dances, and displays of Indian jewelry and crafts.

Area Attractions

Red Rock State Park, situated in Indian Country, is the gateway to Zuni, one of the Seven Cities of Cibola sought by Coronado and the Conquistadors. Also nearbny are Acoma, the sky city, one of the oldest inhabited cities in the United States; Old Laguna Pueblo and its Spanish church; and the Hopi Reservation. The Navajo de Chelly, Chaco Canyon, Aztec Ruins, Navajo and El Morro are among the national monuments within a two-hour drive from Red Rock State Park.

Petrified Forest National Park, the Ice Caves beneath lava Badlands, and the incomparable views of the Badland formations known as the Painted Desert are all natural wonders that shouldn't be missed when exploring the Gallup area.

Annual Events

APRIL:	Square Dance Festi-Gal
JUNE:	Red Rock Team Roping Classic
	(1st weekend)
	Lions Club Rodeo
	(third week and weekend)
JULY:	July 4th Festivities
	Red Rock State Park Pro Rodeo
	(last weekend)
AUGUST:	Inter-tribal Indian Ceremonial
	(second weekend)
DECEMBER:	Red Rock Balloon Festival

The annual Lions Club Rodeo is ranked with the best in the state of New Mexico. In addition, the non-profit Community Concerts organization, as well as the Gallup Gallery, host a variety of concerts during the year at Red Rock State Park.

Camping

The campground has space for 100 units and offers visitors a secluded and breathtaking view of the red rocks.

Activities

The park is set among beautiful red sandstone cliffs that extend up the base of magnificent Church Rock. A walk to the rock is perfect for hiking, picnicking and horseback riding.

Red Rock Museum offers visitors a glimpse of the past and a vision of the enchantment that is New Mexico. Through exhibits on the prehistoric Anasazi and the present-day Zuni, Hopi and Navajo, the museum interprets the unique cultures of the native Americans of the region. It also shows some of the finest traditional works made by local artists.

Outdoor wildflower gardens are ablaze in color from June to September. During the summer months, corn, beans, and squash are grown in a Pueblo "waffle garden," a traditional method of agriculture in the area.

The arena is home to many rodeos each year as well as other events.

An auditorium is the scene of musical events, school programs, city functions, barbecues, weddings, dinners, club luncheons, and fund-raising events. It is an excellent place for visitors to seek entertainment, or to meet local people.

There's also a century-old trading post, a post office, horse stables, and a theater.

For further information contact the Park Superintendent, ☎ (505) 722-3839.

Rio Grande Gorge State Park

Location: 16 miles southwest of Taos on SR 68.

From the Colorado border south to the Taos Junction Bridge on SR 96, is the Rio Grande River. For much of this 48-mile journey, the river is at the bottom of a 1,000-foot gorge, inaccessible from above. The state park is downstream from the bridge, where the gorge broadens into a canyon. A paved road offers a scenic five-mile drive beside the river. Clusters of campsites, some with ramadas (open shelters with slat roofs), are spaced along the road.

The canyon walls are moderately steep, sparsely vegetated, and littered with red-brown volcanic rocks ranging in size from pebbles to boulders. Anyone in good shape and in search of a challenge can scramble up.

The park offers 46 camping sites as well as rafting. If the flow is too low for floating the whitewater section above the gorge, you can always head south of the bridge for a relaxing trip downriver.

For further information contact the Park Superintendent, Rio Grande Gorge State Park, ☎ (505) 827-7899.

North-Central New Mexico

Hyde Memorial State Park

Location: 12 miles northeast of Santa Fe via Hyde Park Road and NM 475.

E njoy camping and picnicking among towering pines and aspen trees. Located near the Santa Fe Ski Basin, the park is also used as a base for backpackers and hikers.

Hyde Memorial State Park, named after Benjamin Talbot Babbit Hyde, is New Mexico's highest, at 8,500 feet. The 350-acre heavily forested park is open year-round, accessible by New Mexico 475 leading to the Santa Fe Ski Basin, approximately eight miles northeast of the Santa Fe Plaza. The beautiful scenery, quiet natural setting, and easy access make Hyde Park a favorite picnic area, campground, respite, as well as a base camp for excursions into the surrounding Santa Fe National Forest.

There are more than 75 camping and picnicking sites nestled throughout the park. These are furnished with picnic tables, fire pits, and grills. Water taps service each group of campsites. Numerous three-sided Adirondack shelters are available off the main road, in addition to seven sites with electric hookups. Sanitary facilities are scattered throughout the park.

The park also has two attractive group picnic shelters that will accommodate 75-100 people. These are used for weddings, reunions, retreats and conferences throughout the year. Reservations may be made by contacting the park at ☎ (505) 983-7175.

In the park's central area is a large children's playground with swing set and slide. Three well-marked hiking trails wind through the remote sections of the park, offering breathtaking views of the surrounding Sangre de Cristo Mountains. Two of these connect with Santa Fe National Forest trails. During the winter months, heavy snowfall makes Hyde Park an excellent destination for winter campers, ski enthusiasts, and outdoor survivalists. There are two well-maintained sledding runs.

At the park's entrance, there is a ranger's office, a general store, information center and, in the winter, a ski rental and repair shop. Close behind sit the elegant old **La Hacienda De-Venado**, a restaurant which is also open year-round.

History

Benjamin Hyde, affectionately known as "Uncle Bennie," was a naturalist, born in New York City in 1872. His early work as a pioneering archeologist and anthropologist brought him to the Southwest, where he became involved in major excavations.

Uncle Bennie is better remembered, however, as a devoted educator of youth. His dedication to the physical, emotional and moral development of youth through natural science and outdoor survival can be appreciated by the countless numbers of people who remember "Uncle Bennie" and his involvement with outdoor life: He served as the National Commissioner of Nature Study for the Boy Scouts of America; he established the Children's Nature Foundation, which purchased hundreds of mountainside acres for the people of Santa Fe; and educated countless youth, introducing them to the wonders of the natural world. A bronze plaque set in a huge boulder at the park's entrance gives tribute to this man's dedication.

> *"Forever serving the youth of America in stimulating love of outdoor life and nature lore."*

Uncle Bennie died in Santa Fe on July 27, 1933. His widow, Mrs. Helen Chauncey Hyde, bequeathed the land now known as Hyde Memorial State Park, with the intention that this park serve the youth of America.

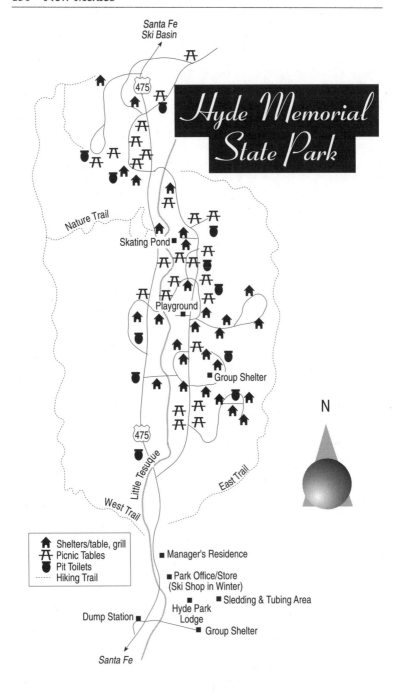

Santa Fe
Ski Basin

475

Hyde Memorial
State Park

Nature Trail

Skating Pond

Playground

Group Shelter

475

Little Tesuque

West Trail

East Trail

N

Shelters/table, grill
Picnic Tables
Pit Toilets
Hiking Trail

Manager's Residence

Park Office/Store
(Ski Shop in Winter)

Sledding & Tubing Area

Hyde Park
Lodge

Dump Station

Group Shelter

Santa Fe

Natural History

Hyde Memorial State Park lies in the Sangre de Cristo Mountains. The Little Tesuque River courses gently through it and small waterfalls drain the snow-capped peaks. The Sangre de Cristos are part of the southern Rocky Mountains and consist primarily of crystalline rock. Altitudes in the park range from 8-10,000 feet.

Since no hunting is permitted here, it is a natural refuge for wildlife. Birds may be heard and seen throughout the park. There are also numerous butterflies. Endangered species which have been spotted in the area include the bald eagle and peregrine falcon.

The unique beauty and diversity of the park's plants and wildlife make Hyde Park an unforgettable reminder of this land's complex, fragile ecosystem. It encourages understanding and appreciation of this irreplaceable part of earth's natural wonders.

Trails

The Nature Interpretive Trail: A half-mile well-marked trail with signs to identify various plants, trees and wildflowers found along the way. This trail is halfway between the entrance and exit of the park off NM 475 on the northwest side, easily identified by a plaque.

West Trail: The south end of this three-mile trail is located directly across the road from the ranger's residence. The trail runs north to the RV campsite area. This strenuous hike, gaining 1,000 feet in elevation, offers panoramic views of the Sangre de Cristo, Sandia, and Jemez Mountain ranges, the City of Santa Fe and the Santa Fe Ski Basin. Trees, shrubs, wildflowers and plants abound. Along the upper ridge of the trail hikers will find picnic tables and log benches. There are steep elevations and rocky downhill sections. Sturdy shoes and drinking water are a must. The trail connects with the nature trail and Santa Fe National Forest trails.

East Trail: A remote, moderately hilly 1.5-mile trail snuggled in the dense ponderosa pines. The trail starts toward the northeast end of the park across the road from the RV area and ends near the ranger station. It is marked by a small "hiker" sign.

Canyon Trail: A 0.5-mile steep canyon excursion trail leads to one of the park's beautiful waterfalls. It starts behind Group Shelter 2. Great caution must be used as this area is slick and rocky. It also connects with the Santa Fe National Forest Trails.

For additional information contact: Hyde Memorial State Park, PO Box 1147, Santa Fe, NM 87504-1147. ☎ (505) 983-7175.

Santa Fe River State Park

Location: In downtown Santa Fe along the Santa Fe River.

Tree-lined walkways and picnic tables stretch along this narrow portion of the Santa Fe River.

For further information contact the Park Superintendent, Santa Fe River State Park, PO Box 1147, Santa Fe, NM 87504. ☎ (505) 827-7465.

Northeast New Mexico

Chicosa State Park

Location: 9 miles northeast of Roy via NM 120.

This small high plains park includes historical exhibits and photographs of area cattle drives along the Goodnight-Loving Trail.

For further information, ☎ (505) 485-2424.

Cimarron Canyon State Park
(Colin Neblett Wildlife Area)

Location: 3 miles east of Eagle Nest via US 64.

Cimarron Canyon is a forested area set between the towns of Eagle Nest and Ute Park, New Mexico. It offers opportunities for camping, hiking, fishing, and hunting. US Highway 64, which runs through the canyon, provides easy access to the Cimarron River.

The park is part of the Colin Neblett Wildlife Area, but there are some additional regulations that are unique to this area. The first of these is that at least one member of each camping party must have a current New Mexico hunting or fishing license. One night's free camping is given with each valid license. The license requirement was put into place because, being a state wildlife area, the facilities were all originally purchased and developed with fish and wildlife funds. Another strictly-enforced regulation is that camping and vehicles are allowed only in designated and developed areas. There are also some designated "Quality Fishing Waters" within the park that have their own regulations. Call for details.

The park has about 100 developed sites and nine tent-only sites. Generally, to get a good site it is best to arrive by mid-day on a weekday. Weekends and holidays are usually very busy and the grounds fill up early.

For further information contact Colin Neblett Wildlife Area, c/o New Mexico Dept. of Game & Fish, PO Box 25112, Santa Fe, NM 87504. ☎ (505) 827-7882.

Clayton Lake State Park

Location: 15 miles north of Clayton via NM 370.

Set among rolling grasslands, the stocked lake offers excellent trout, catfish and bass fishing. In the winter, the lake is closed to fishing and provides a magnificent stopover for migrating waterfowl. The sight of these birds is well worth the trip. A short trail overlooks a rare 100-million-year-old dinosaur trackway, containing nearly 500 footprints.

The lake, about three-quarters of a mile long, is irregular in shape, with some rock bluffs along the shore. Boats are limited to trolling speed. It's possible to hike around the lake, but there are no marked trails. Hunters are often found camping in this area.

Campsites are attractively scattered all along the southern shore. There are 78 sites available all year. With the nearest town of significant population being over 100 miles away, you can be fairly certain to get a site here!

For further information contact the Park Superintendent, Clayton Lake State Park, Clayton, NM 88415. ☎ (505) 374-8808.

Colin Neblett Wildlife Area

Location: Both sides of US 64, between Cimarron and Eagle Nest.

This is New Mexico's largest wildlife area. The canyon is not narrow, although several sections have vertical cliffs with sculptured formations that attract both photographers and climbers. There are two main tributaries running through here: Tolby Creek and Clear Creek. The upper portion of Clear Creek has three eight-foot waterfalls.

About three-quarters of the area is heavily forested. Cottonwood and aspen are prominent on the bottomland, ponderosa pine and juniper dot the sloping canyon walls.

Camping along the highway is permitted only in designated areas. The camp areas offer a total of 80 sites and are managed and maintained by the Park and Recreation Division. An unusual provision is that campers must have valid New Mexico hunting or fishing licenses. The sites are often filled on weekends and are open throughout the year.

Except for hunters, few people visit the backcountry. The terrain is a little rough for novices. All backcountry roads and tracks have been closed to vehicles, but hiking and backpacking are popular with numerous unmarked trails throughout the area. Hunters will find deer, elk, bear, mountain lion, turkey, grouse, while fishermen will enjoy rainbow and brown trout.

For further information contact Colin Neblett Wildlife Area, c/o New Mexico Dept. of Game & Fish, PO Box 25112, Santa Fe, NM 87504. ☎ (505) 827-7882.

Conchas Lake State Park

Location: 34 miles northwest of Tucumcari via NM 104.

$\mathcal{W}$ater sports abound, including boating, fishing and waterskiing at this refreshing 25-mile-long reservoir.

For further information contact the Park Superintendent, Conchas Lake State Park, PO Box 976, Conchas Dam, NM 88416. ☎ (505) 868-2270.

Coyote Creek State Park

Location: 14 miles north of Mora via NM 434.

$\mathcal{T}$his secluded park is nestled in the Sangre de Cristo Mountains along a meandering stream where visitors can fish for rainbow and brown trout.

The park is small and surrounded by private land, but it seems spacious. In the foothills of the Sangre de Cristos, the park sits in a natural amphitheater formed by low hills around the creek's flood plain. Slopes are forested with ponderosa pine and pinyon-juniper. Cottonwood, willow, and tamarisk can be found on the flood plain, along with abundant wildflowers. The creek is shallow and varies between five and 15 feet in width.

Camping is informal. A few sites have shelters, but people camp wherever they find a level spot. A one-mile trail begins at the group campsite, ascends to the ridge, and returns.

For further information contact the Park Superintendent, Coyote Creek State Park, Mora, NM 87714. ☎ (505) 387-2328.

Morphy Lake State Park

Location: 4 miles south of Mora via NM 94, 7 miles west of Ledoux.

This undeveloped area is accessible by foot, horseback or four-wheel-drive vehicle. The small scenic lake is stocked with trout, and boating is limited to electric motors. **Note:** Visitors should bring their own drinking water.

For further information contact the Park Superintendent, Morphy Lake State Park, Mora, NM 87504. ☎ (505) 387-2328.

Santa Rosa Lake State Park

Location: From Santa Rosa on I-40, head out 8th St. and go 7 miles due north.

The Corps of Engineers dammed the Pecos River here for irrigation and flood control, completing the main embankment in 1981. At full pool the reservoir has a surface area of 12,294 acres. The lake attracts many boaters and campers when the water is high enough.

The park has a short "scenic trail." Hiking opportunities are greater when the water surface is low, exposing land along the old river channel and canyon.

Activities in Santa Rosa Lake State Park include 48 campsites plus numerous primitive sites. Hunting is permitted just outside of the park boundaries where dove, quail and waterfowl are abundant.

For further information contact the Park Superintendent, Santa Rosa State Park, Santa Rosa, NM 88418. ☎ (505) 472-3115.

Storrie Lake State Park

Location: 4 miles north of Las Vegas via NM 518.

Favorable summer breezes attract colorful windsurfing boats to this park, which is also popular for fishing and boating. The visitor center features historical exhibits on the Santa Fe Trail and 19th-century Las Vegas.

History

The area surrounding Las Vegas was occupied as early as 8000 B.C. by Paleo-Indians. In more recent times, Pueblo Indians, nomadic Plains Indians, Comanches, Spanish explorers and settlers lived in or passed through the area.

The town of Las Vegas was established in 1835, when a small group of settlers received a land grant from the Mexican government. The town flourished throughout the 1800s' due to its proximity to the Santa Fe Trail, which was used by pioneers and traders heading west. The introduction of rail service by the Santa Fe Railroad in 1879 contributed further to the town's growth and prosperity.

The town attracted not only traders and settlers, but also notorious outlaws. In 1879, the famed gunslinger and dentist, Doc Holliday, opened a dental office and saloon in the town. It is said he devoted much of his time to gambling, drinking and fighting. Other infamous figures, including Billy the Kid and Jesse James, were drawn to the freewheeling Las Vegas of the 1880's. By the turn of the century, however, the outlaw influence had declined and merchants and traders established many new businesses. The Las Vegas of today reflects its colorful and unique past.

Some of the rock formations surrounding Storrie Lake are more than 90 million years old, dating from the Cretaceous Period. They are made up of shales, siltstones, limestones, and sandstones which were deposited at the bottom of a warm shallow sea at the time New Mexico was mostly covered by seawater.

Fossils found in the Storrie Lake area include squid, octopi, and ammonites, extinct relatives of today's nautilus. Ammonoids swam and hunted food in the shallow Cretaceous seas. They became extinct at the same time as dinosaurs, about 66 million years ago. A large ammonite fossil is on display at the park visitor center.

In 1916, contractor Robert Storrie began work on a 1,400-foot-long earthfill dam across the Gallinas River north of Las Vegas to provide irrigation water for neighboring vegetable farms. Financial problems plagued the project and farmers failed to produce the anticipated crops due to harsh and unpredictable weather. The

Storrie Lake Water Users Association assumed management of the project in 1944. Although attempts to develop a productive agricultural area continued, Storrie Lake was dedicated a state park in 1960.

Activities

Storrie Lake State Park, at 6,430 feet elevation, is situated on 82 acres. The lake contains approximately 1,100 surface acres of water and is well known for its year-round fishing for rainbow and German brown trout and crappie. A state fishing license is required.

Conditions are excellent for windsurfing and sailboarding due to steady breezes most of the summer. Sailboarders flock to regattas and tournaments during these months. waterskiing is also popular at Storrie Lake.

Facilities

The park campground features 11 sites with electricity and water hookups, and 21 picnic tables with shelters and grills. Primitive camping is also available, and the park has restrooms with hot showers, a sump station and potable water. A fee is charged for both day use and overnight camping. Park gates are locked at sunset.

Plants & Animals

The plants around Storrie Lake are typical of the High Plains country. The dryness of the area is emphasized by the abundance of cholla, prickly pear, and several other varieties of cacti.

Storrie Lake attracts waterfowl, especially during the late fall and winter migration.

For further information contact the Park Superintendent, Storrie Lake State Park, PO Box 3157, Las Vegas, NM 87701. ☎ (505) 425-7278.

Sugarite Canyon State Park

Location: 10 miles northeast of Raton via NM 526.

This unique park, located on the border of Colorado, features heavily wooded mountains and meadows painted with wildflowers. It is popular in the winter for ice-fishing and cross-country skiing. The park includes extensive historical and nature exhibits. No gasoline motors are allowed on the lakes.

For further information contact the Park Superintendent, Sugarite Canyon State Park, Raton, NM 88415. ☎ (505) 445-5607.

Ute Lake State Park

Location: 3 miles west of Logan via NM 540.

Some of the best walleye fishing in New Mexico is found at this Canadian River reservoir, where anglers try their luck for bass, crappie, and catfish.

For further information contact the Park Superintendent, Ute Lake State Park, Logan, NM 88401. ☎ (505) 487-2284.

Villaneuva State Park

Location: 31 miles southwest of Las Vegas via I-25 and NM 3.

Nestled between high red sandstone bluffs along the Pecos River near the picturesque Spanish-colonial village of Villaneuva, the park includes hiking trails with views of old ranching ruins and fishing. Short trails follow the river and ascend the bluffs to a lookout.

An attractive 77-site campground (open year-round) is set between the sandstone bluffs on the Pecos River. The shallow river here is about 30 feet wide and has a moderately swift flow. The tan to reddish bluffs reach over 150 feet high. Cottonwoods grow near the river. Slopes are dotted with pinyon-juniper.

The road from the interstate is quiet, often close to the river, passing through old Spanish towns where adobe houses are being replaced by mobile homes.

For further information contact the Park Superintendent at ☎ (505) 421-2957.

Southeast New Mexico

Bottomless Lakes State Park

Location: 16 miles southeast of Roswell via US 380 and NM 409.

The beautiful and unique area known as Bottomless Lakes State Park comes as a complete surprise after the flat country surrounding Roswell, New Mexico. Dropping down from the bluffs, the access road loops around seven lakes. These lakes, actually sinkholes ranging in depth from 17 feet to 90 feet, were formed when circulating underground water dissolved salt and gypsum deposits to form subterranean caverns. When the roofs of the caverns collapsed from their own weight, sinkholes resulted and soon filled with water. The illusion of great depth and the greenish-blue color are created by algae and other aquatic plants covering the lake bottoms.

In the 1800's, the lakes were a stopover for cowboys herding cattle through the New Mexico territory on the Goodnight-Loving Trail. After they tried without success to find the bottom of the lakes with their lariats tied together, they dubbed the lakes "bottomless." The lariats were actually swept aside by underwater currents.

Bottomless Lakes State Park was dedicated in 1933, the first area set aside as a state park in New Mexico. The original stone structure at Lea Lake was built by the Civilian Conservation Corps in 1934 and 1935. The park offers a variety of sports, including hiking, swimming, fishing, and scuba diving.

This area is also known for "Pecos Diamonds," which are actually quartz crystals formed inside gypsum. The soft gypsum sometimes crumbles away exposing the "diamonds."

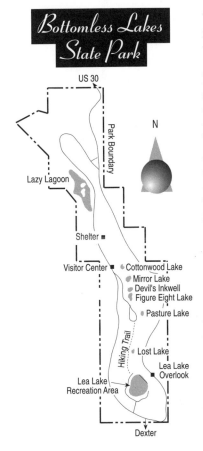

The lakes which give this park its name are located along the west side road.

Lazy Lagoon looks deceptively shallow but is actually 90 feet deep. It is surrounded by treacherous alkaline mud flats. The crust covers deep, unpleasant smelling mud. Visitors should not attempt to walk or drive near this muddy area. In the fall, winter, and spring, flocks of waterfowl are often seen here.

Cottonwood Lake is 30 feet deep and was named for a large cottonwood tree that once stood on its shore. The park visitor center is located here with exhibits describing the natural history of the area. A nature trail leads from the center through "Lake in the Making" and on to a scenic view of Mirror Lake. Rainbow trout are stocked here during the winter.

Mirror Lake is 50 feet deep and was, until recently, two ponds separated by a narrow strip of land. The northern pond of Mirror Lake was too salty for game fish while the smaller southern pond was less alkaline and able to support fish. Today, the two ponds form a single lake which is stocked with rainbow trout. It is aptly named for its beautiful reflection of the surrounding red bluffs.

Devil's Inkwell is 32 feet deep and is named for its steep sides and very dark water, the result of algae growth. Overnight campsites and drinking water are available nearby. A short hike to a vantage point above the lake is well worth the effort. Rainbow trout are also stocked in this lake during the winter.

Figure Eight Lake is actually two contiguous sinkholes 37 feet deep. This is a quiet lake bordered by numerous salt cedar trees.

Pasture Lake, at 17 feet deep, is the shallowest of the lakes. Nearby Picnic Dell is a dry sinkhole that illustrates how the lakes were formed.

Lea Lake is 90 feet deep and the largest of the Bottomless Lakes. It is the only lake in which swimming is allowed. During the summer months, the park operates a concession stand where pedal cruisers and paddleboards are available for a nominal fee. A bath house with hot showers and flush toilets is near the concession area. The lake is spring fed with almost 2½ million gallons of water flowing through it daily. Due to the clarity of the water in Lea Lake, scuba diving has become very popular.

Camping

Roomy campsites are available, both at Lea Lake Recreation Area and along the lower lakes. The lower lakes offer developed camping with centralized fresh water and chemical toilets. Lea Lake offers full hookups with modern restrooms and hot showers. There is a large day use and picnic area adjacent to the lake. The swimming beach is well maintained and lifeguards are on duty during the summer. Entrance and camping fees are charged throughout the year.

For more information contact: Bottomless Lakes State Park, H C 12, Box 1200, Roswell, NM 88201. ☎ (505) 624-6058.

Living Desert State Park

Location: In northwest Carlsbad off US 285.

The park is an indoor/outdoor living museum displaying more than 40 native animal species and hundreds of succulents from around the world. Exhibits include an aviary, nocturnal house, botanical garden, and enclosures for reptiles, hoofed animals, and other creatures.

For further information contact the Park Superintendent, Living Desert State Park, carlsbad, NM 88240. ☎ (505) 887-5516.

Harry McAdams State Park

Location: 4 miles northwest of Hobbs via NM 18.

This extensively landscaped park offers cool greenery surrounding a pair of small ponds.

Harry McAdams State Park is named for the New Mexico State Senator whose efforts were instrumental in the creation of this new facility, formerly known as Lea County State Park. It is the first state park in Lea County.

Development of Harry McAdams State Park was funded by $1.5 million appropriated by the New Mexico Legislature in 1977 and 1980. Facilities include a visitor center with interpretive exhibits describing the natural and human histories of the Hobbs region, a park manager's residence and maintenance facility, a campground with 15 RV sites equipped with electrical hookups, a recreational vehicle sanitary dump station, 10 picnic shelters, a comfort station with showers and handicapped access, a playground, and a multiple-use ball field. The park's 35 acres are irrigated and extensively landscaped.

For further information contact the Park Superintendent, Harry McAdams State Park, Hobbs, NM 88240. ☎ (505) 392-5845.

Sumner Lake State Park

Location: 16 miles northwest of Fort Sumner via US 84 and NM 203.

Sumner Lake is stocked with bass, crappie and channel catfish, and is a winter haven for migrating waterfowl.

For further information contact the Park Superintendent, Sumner Lake State Park, Fort Sumner, NM 88317. ☎ (505) 355-2541.

Oasis State Park

Location: 18 miles north of Portales via NM 467.

A true oasis, this park is set among cottonwood trees, shifting sand dunes, and a small fishing lake.

For further information contact the Park Superintendent, Oasis State Park, Portales, NM 88101. ☎ (505) 356-5331.

Oliver Lee Memorial State Park

Location: 10 miles south of Alamogordo via US 54.

Set against the west-facing escarpment of the Sacramento Mountains, the park features historical exhibits and a fully restored 19th-century ranch house. Springs from Dog Canyon support a variety of unexpected plant life, including maidenhair fern and wild orchids.

Named for Oliver Milton Lee, a pioneer southern New Mexico rancher and state legislator, Oliver Lee Memorial State Park is at the mouth of Dog Canyon in the rugged Sacramento Mountains. Water flows year-round in Dog Canyon, creating a quiet green oasis in contrast to the surrounding prickly desert setting. For many centuries people have been drawn to this place of surprising beauty.

History

Oliver Milton Lee was born in Texas on November 8, 1865. At the age of 19, he and his half-brother brought their livestock from Texas to the area, establishing his ranch headquarters at Dog Canyon in 1893.

As his New Mexico land holdings and influence grew, Lee faced more and more competition for the use of open rangeland. He became embroiled in the violent political rivalries between the predominantly Republican early settlers of southern New Mexico and the Democrat newcomers from Texas. Intermittent hostilities led to several indictments against Lee, including one in 1896 for the murder of a prominent New Mexican, Col. A. J. Fountain. The evidence against Lee proved to be circumstantial and, in 1899, he was acquitted of the murder charge.

In 1914, Lee was part of a group that created the Cirde Cross Cattle Company. It soon became the largest ranching enterprise in southern New Mexico, controlling nearly one million acres of ranch land from Cloudcroft, New Mexico to El Paso, Texas. Although financial troubles in the 1920s forced dissolution of the company, Lee continued ranching. For many years, he was active in state and local politics, serving in both houses of the New Mexico State Legislature during his political career. His death in 1941 marked the end of one of the most colorful careers in New Mexico history. Oliver Lee Memorial State Park commemorates the life and times of this important New Mexico pioneer.

Oliver Lee's Dog Canyon ranch headquarters has been completely rebuilt from ruins and is authentically furnished. Some of the everyday items the Lee family used during their residency from 1893 to 1907 are also on display, including marbles, coins, cartridge casings, bottles, china doll fragments, dining utensils, poker chips, and sewing notions. Ruins of the barn, corrals, and chicken house still remain, and Lee's extensive orchard and vineyard has been started up again.

Planners utilized various historic photographs, archeological evidence, and first-hand accounts from former residents in developing the reconstruction plans. Visitors to Oliver Lee Memorial State Park can journey back in time to the days of this influential rancher during regularly scheduled guided tours of the house.

The availability of water, combined with the ease of defense of this natural fortress, made Dog Canyon a haven for the wandering aboriginal populations of southern New Mexico, who used the canyon's perennial springs as a stopover campsite.

Archeological research indicates that, more than 4,000 years ago, the trail through Dog Canyon was used as a route for groups of people moving from the lowland desert into the Sacramento and Guadalupe Mountains.

The prehistoric inhabitants of the southwest were adept at identifying appropriate materials for the stone tools that were an integral part of their daily lives. Many different types of glass-like rock – easily chipped and flaked to produce a sharp cutting edge – have been found in the outcroppings of the canyon walls. Nearly 170,000 stone artifacts, including hammer stones, scrapers, drills, gouges, and knives, have been found in Dog Canyon. The most prominent remains are mortars used by prehistoric Indians to grind hard seeds, such as mesquite. These cylindrical holes were formed in boulders and canyon bedrock by the continual pounding of hand-held pestles. Sometimes called "Indian wells" because of their tendency to collect and hold rainwater, these signs of ancient civilizations are scattered throughout the site.

Historians believe the fierce, nomadic Apache Indians first came to Dog Canyon approximately 500 years ago as part of a general southward migration of Indian tribes from central Canada. The strong Apache presence in the Sacramento Mountains prevented Spanish and Anglo settlement of the area until the late 19th century.

The Apaches used Dog Canyon as a fortress. Below the narrow "eyebrow" trail, which hugs the edge of a steep 2,000-foot bluff, the canyon forms a natural trap where enemies were lured and then bombarded with rocks and boulders.

Numerous US Army military reports from the period between 1849 and 1881 document Apache raids in southern New Mexico and Texas. In many cases the raiders were tracked across the Tularosa Basin to Dog Canyon, which provided a route of quick escape to the east.

It was not until the 1870's that large-scale raiding came to an end. Once the Apache threat was under control, a wave of settlers arrived and a new phase of history began at Dog Canyon.

Francois-Jean "Frenchy" Rochas, born in France in 1843, emigrated to New Mexico in the mid-1880s. This unshakable, solitary Frenchman homesteaded at the mouth of Dog Canyon near Alamogordo for almost a decade, raising cattle and cultivating an orchard and vineyard on the site of what is now Oliver Lee Memorial State Park.

Experts believe that, in about 1893, Frenchy and Oliver Lee built a cement flume on the south wall of Dog Canyon to channel water across the Frenchman's homestead to Lee's ranch headquarters a mile away. Vestiges of this irrigation system still exist and, in a letter composed just before his death, Rochas described the extensive garden it once watered: "I am working on my vineyard. I have also put out some trees, some olives, some figs, apple, cherry, plum, peach, so as to have a little of everything."

Frenchy's good fortune ended abruptly soon after Christmas 1894, when he was found dead in his cabin, shot through the chest. Although a coroner's jury concluded that Frenchy shot himself with his own rifle, it seems more likely that he was murdered by cattlemen who owed him money. The mystery of the Frenchman's death has never been solved.

Excavation around the cabin produced an unexpected wealth of materials that helped fill in the outlines of Frenchy's existence at Dog Canyon. Archeologists found bottles for alcoholic beverages and medicines, tin cans, boots, a lamp burner, a lock, cartridge casings, and other telltale clues that give color and substance to the Frenchman's story. Park visitors can view a partial reconstruction of Frenchy's two-room home as well as the stone walls he built to corral his livestock.

Features

Today's visitors enjoy the park's fascinating natural and human history through extensive exhibits in the park's visitor center and interpretive trails. The park is open year-round and is well-equipped to accommodate overnight and day-use visitors with 44 developed picnic/campsites. Seventeen of these sites have electric hookups and shelters, with water readily available in the campground. A restroom with showers and a recreational vehicle dump station are within the campground.

Dog Canyon – Canon del Perro – is one of many deep canyons that gash the west-facing flank of the Sacramento Mountains as they stretch through southern New Mexico. Located midway in the rugged, 35-mile-long Sacramento Mountain Escarpment, the canyon wall rises abruptly more than 2,000 feet from the arid floor of the Tularosa Basin to the rocks that mark the canyon's head. Its jutting walls exhibit strata of dolomite, siltstone, limestone, sandstone, and shale.

Plants & Animals

A stream runs year-round through the canyon in this region that normally receives less than 10 inches of precipitation annually. The freshwater springs in the canyon walls support a lush greenery that is unexpected among the desert yucca, mesquite, and prickly pear found beyond the canyon's confines. The riparian (streambed) plant community is typified by a thick canopy of cottonwoods and ash, with delicate maidenhair ferns clinging to moist rock walls and orchids growing in the stream.

Just as the plant life in Dog Canyon is remarkably diverse and beautiful, the canyon is also the habitat for a wide assortment of birds, mammals, and reptiles. Characteristic desert birds such as the cactus wren, the roadrunner (New Mexico's state bird), and mockingbird are found here, along with quail, warblers and sparrows. The peregrine falcon, an endangered species, has also been sighted in the vicinity. Deer, coyotes, foxes, ringtail cats, rabbits, and mountain lions live in the canyon, and a variety of lizards and snakes are also commonly seen.

In the sun-scorched country of the Tularosa Basin, Dog Canyon is an oasis of delicately balanced life, set like a lush green gem in an otherwise harsh and arid land.

Dog Canyon National Recreational Trail

This is a 4.2-mile hike that departs from the Oliver Lee visitor center and ends on Forest Road 90B at Joplin Ridge. Visitors will not be breaking any new ground by hiking the trail, as prehistoric Indians used the path to travel from the Tularosa Basin to the Sacramento Mountains for thousands of years.

Sturdy shoes and drinking water are essential for the dry, strenuous walk that gains more than 3,000 feet in elevation. It is worth the effort, however, to experience the panoramic views of the Tularosa Basin and the glimmering White Sands National Monument. On the upper rock bench, hikers pass through a thickly carpeted grassland interspersed with cottonwoods, willow, and ash. The cool oasis of a small creek is found about 2.4 miles from the start of the trail. Spring and autumn are the best times to attempt this hike because of intense summer heat and unpredictable winter weather.

For further information contact the Oliver Lee Memorial State Park, 409 Dog Canyon Road, Alamogordo, NM 88310. ☎ (505) 437-8284.

Smokey Bear Historical State Park

Location: In Capitan on US 380.

This park celebrates the life and legacy of America's most famous bear. The visitor center includes extensive exhibits on Smokey Bear and wildfire education. A short nature trail winds through various New Mexico life zones to the site where the original Smokey is buried.

For further information contact the Park Superintendent, Smokey Bear Historical State Park, Capitan, NM 88316. ☎ (505) 354-2748.

Brantley Lake State Park

Location: 12 miles north of Carlsbad via US 285.

This southern desert park is a refreshing place to fish and enjoy other water sports. The visitor center includes historical exhibits about the Wild West town of Seven Rivers.

For further information contact the Park Superintendent, Brantley Lake State Park, Carlsbad, NM 88220. ☎ (505) 457-2384.

Valley Of Fires State Park

Location: On US 380, 1 mile west of Carrizozo.

The fires are long since out. The park overlooks the Carrizozo Lava Flow – one of the youngest lava flows of the continent, occurring 1,500 to 2,000 years ago. The lava flow has a variety of interesting formations, though no features as dramatic as the lava tubes and ice caves of El Malpais in Zone 1. Windblown soil has settled in crevices, and a variety of colonizing plants have taken root. These in turn support modest wildlife populations, chiefly small mammals and their predators.

A nature trail leads from the group campground for three-quarters of a mile through the nearby lava field. An exhibit stands at the beginning of the trail.

There are 50 campsites available for year-round use.

Note: Don't even think of trying to hike on lava in ordinary foot-gear. Sharp edges cut and rough surfaces are everywhere!

Contact Superintendent, Valley of Fire State Park, Carrizozo, NM 88301.

Southwest New Mexico

Caballo Lake State Park

Location: 16 miles south of Truth or Consequences via I-25.

The Caballo Mountains serve as a majestic backdrop to the lake, which boasts a full array of water sports, winter waterfowl and cactus gardens.

For further information contact the Park Superintendent, Caballa Lake State Park,truth or Consequences, NM 87901. ☎ (505) 743-3942.

Percha Dam State Park

Location: 21 miles south of Truth or Consequences via I-25.

Set in the deep shade of towering cottonwoods, the park features fishing and hiking along the Rio Grande.

For further information contact the Park Superintendent, Percha Dam State Park, Truth or Consequences, NM 87903. ☎ (505) 743-3942.

Elephant Butte Lake State Park

Location: 5 miles north of Truth or Consequences via I-25.

Set in the lower Rio Grande Valley of southcentral New Mexico, Elephant Butte Lake State Park is the largest and most popular state park in New Mexico. Elephant Butte Reservoir, created by a dam constructed in 1916 across the Rio Grande, is 40 miles long with more that 200 miles of shoreline. The 36,000 surface-acre reservoir offers a vast array of water sports, including boating, fishing and waterskiing. The park has over 200 camping and picnicking sites. There are three developed boat ramps on the lake, along with concession-operated marinas and stores.

Elephant Butte Lake State Park first opened in 1965. Mild climates create a haven for campers from cooler northern climates during the winter months. Boating and fishing are popular all year.

History: Elephants at Elephant Butte?

Fossils of the stegomastodon, a primitive relative of today's elephant, have been discovered on land just west of the Elephant Butte Reservoir. Shorter and stockier than the Asian elephants, the animal was seven feet tall, with a short skull and long upper tusks. Although these elephant-like creatures once roamed the area, Elephant Butte was not named for this reason. The eroded core of an ancient volcano, now an island in the reservoir, has taken on the shape of an elephant.

The region has been an important center of settlement for thousands of years. Until 1000 A.D., the area was occupied by Indian groups, who appear to have lived primarily by hunting and gathering the abundant wildlife and plants of the surrounding valleys and mountains. Over time, several different groups lived in the area.

During the massive immigration of European settlers into the West in the early 19th century, the threat of Indian attacks along the Rio Grande Valley made the settlers reluctant to put down roots in the area. The US military established Fort Conrad, Fort Craig, and Fort McRae in the mid-1800's to protect settlers. Numerous Hispanic agricultural villages sprang up during this time. The construction

Elephant Butte State Park

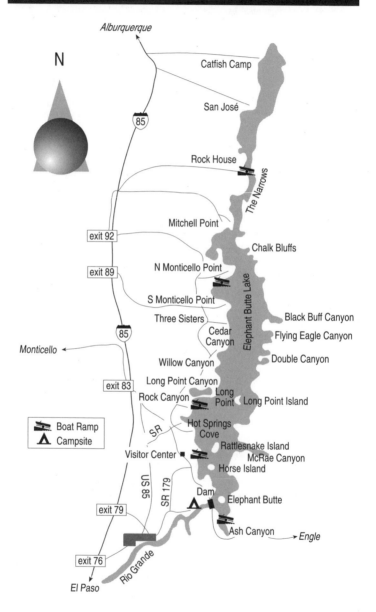

Alburquerque

N

Catfish Camp

San José

85

Rock House

The Narrows

Mitchell Point

exit 92

Chalk Bluffs

exit 89

N Monticello Point

Elephant Butte Lake

S Monticello Point

Three Sisters

Black Buff Canyon

85

Cedar Canyon

Flying Eagle Canyon

Monticello

Willow Canyon

Double Canyon

exit 83

Long Point Canyon

Rock Canyon

Long Point

Long Point Island

SR

Boat Ramp

Campsite

Hot Springs Cove

Visitor Center

Rattlesnake Island

McRae Canyon

Horse Island

US 85

SR 179

Dam

Elephant Butte

exit 79

Ash Canyon

Engle

exit 76

Rio Grande

El Paso

of the dam led to condemnation of many of these settlements, which now lie beneath the waters of the reservoir. A few adobe ruins of old Fort McRae remain on the east side of the reservoir.

Activities

Fishing is probably the most popular year-round sport at Elephant Butte Lake State Park. Game fish include large- and smallmouth bass, striped bass, walleye, channel catfish, crappie, white bass, and bluegill. For birdwatchers, species often sighted include osprey, kestrel, bald eagle, egret, red-tailed hawk, deer, great blue heron, quail, and roadrunners.

For further information contact the Superintendent, Elephant Butte Lake State Park, PO Box 13, Elephant Butte, NM 87935. ☎ (505) 744-5421.

City of Rocks State Park

Location: 28 miles northeast of Deming via US 180 and NM 61.

*V*olcanic rock, sculpted millions of years ago by wind and water into rows of monolithic blocks, gives this park its name. Cactus gardens and hiking trails add to the appeal of this amazing place.

The central feature here is a 40-acre field of large boulders, volcanic rock eroded into fanciful shapes. The park is at 5,000 feet elevation in a desert environment. The attractive 50-site campground has a cultivated cactus garden.

For further information contact the Park Superintendent, City of Rocks State Park, PO Box 54, Faywood, NM 88034. ☎ (505) 536-2800.

Leasburg Dam State Park

Location: 15 miles north of Las Cruces via I-25.

A pleasant park for fishing, canoeing and kayaking, Leasburg Dam channels water from the Rio Grande for irrigation in the

Mesilla Valley. Nearby Fort Selden State Monument has a museum and trails at the site of a 19th-century army outpost.

For further information contact the Park Superintendent, Leasburg Dam State Park, Las Cruces, NM 88091. ☎ (505) 524-4068.

Rockhound State Park

Location: 14 miles southeast of Deming via NM 11 and Road 141.

*L*ocated on the rugged west slope of the Little Florida Mountains, the park is a favorite of rockhounds because of the abundant agates and quartz crystals found here. Hiking trails provide spectacular views of the surrounding landscape.

For further information contact the Park Superintendent, Rockhound State Park, Demington, NM 88231. ☎ (505) 546-6182.

Pancho Villa State Park

Location: 35 miles south of Deming on NM 11.

*I*n the early morning darkness of March 9, 1916, guerillas of the Mexican Revolution under General Francisco "Pancho" Villa attacked the small New Mexico border town and military camp at Columbus – the site of what is now Pancho Villa State Park. As the sun rose, the center of the town was a smoking ruin. News of Pancho Villa's attack flashed by telegraph and word of mouth throughout the country. Camp Furlong, the Columbus military outpost, was buzzing with activity as fresh troops arrived by train and the US Army prepared an attack into Mexico.

Led by "Black Jack" Pershing, who would later command the Allied forces of World War I, the Punitive Expedition forged south from Columbus. The search for Pancho Villa would take the troops nearly 400 miles into Mexico. For 11 months they searched the countryside of Mexico Pancho and his troops.

Pershing succeeded in dispersing the Mexican forces that had attacked Columbus, but the revolutionary chieftain, Pancho Villa, vanished into the backcountry and was never captured. In February, 1917, the American troops returned to Columbus and boarded trains that would carry them to other conflicts.

The military post at Camp Furlong was closed in 1926, and the extensive cactus gardens of Pancho Villa State Park now cover its site. Several of the buildings dating back to the time of the raid still stand, including the adobe Hoover Hotel, the restored Columbus railroad depot, and the old US Customs Building.

For further information contact Pancho Villa State Park, PO Box 224, Columbus, NM 88029. ☎ (505) 531-2711.

Central New Mexico

Coronado State Park

Location: 15 miles north of Albuquerque,
along the Rio Grande in Barnalillo on NM 44.

A visit to Coronado State Park offers more than a place to set up camp or enjoy a picnic. Relax and take in an unobstructed view of the beautiful Sandia mountains to the east. Experience the quiet mystique of the Rio Grande as it flows gently through the valley below. Enjoy New Mexico's spectacular sunrises, and witness the Sandia's reflecting light from the setting sun. Tour the adjacent Coronado State Monument with its Indian artifacts and partially restored Adobe pueblo ruins.

History

In early 1539, an army of Spanish soldiers, Indians, horses, mules, and a traveling food reserve of pigs, chickens and cattle left Compostela, Mexico in search of the legendary City of Gold. Eighteen months later, their travels brought them to the Rio Grande, just north of present day Albuquerque. Instead of golden riches, they found centuries-old Indian villages. After spending the winter in the area, they traveled into Kansas and Oklahoma in their relentless quest. They returned a year later on their way back to Mexico, defeated in their search for power and wealth.

The wintering grounds for Coronado and his 1,200 men were in the vicinity of the Kuaua Pueblo, which is the site of present day Coronado State Monument. This pueblo was among 12 to 14 others in the area which were first settled around A.D. 1300. Excavations of Kuaua indicate the pueblo contained approximately 1,200 ground-level rooms and rose three stories high.

Several hundred people lived in the pueblo at the time of Coronado's arrival. The pueblo dwellers were farmers who grew corn, squash, and beans. They abandoned Kuaua Pueblo in the early 1600s when Spanish colonization of the Rio Grande Valley was underway.

Underground ceremonial chambers, called kivas, were found among the many plazas of the Kuaua Pueblo. One has been restored and is open to public view.

Facilities

Coronado State Park offers picnicking and camping facilities along a bluff above the Rio Grande. There are 30 sites with shelters, two group shelters and many tent sites. There are also two modern restrooms, one with showers, and electric hookups for RVs at 15 of the campsites.

Please observe the following park rules to make your visit safe and enjoyable:

- Observe quiet hours 10 pm to 7 am daily.
- Build fires in grills or designated areas only.
- Keep your pets leashed at all times.
- Keep your campsite neat, clean and sanitary.
- Drive slowly; obey speed limits.

The park gate closes at 10 pm and opens at 7 am daily.

For further information contact the Park Superintendent, Coronado State Park, Barnalillo, NM 87128. ☎ (505) 867-5589.

Coronado State Monument

Location: 15 miles north of Albuquerque,
along the Rio Grande in Barnalillo on NM 44.

The site of Kuaua was designated Coronado State Monument in 1940. The monument offers visitors an opportunity to learn more about pueblo life during the time of Coronado's expedition. Located adjacent to Coronado State Park, it includes an interpretive trail through the partially reconstructed ruins of the pueblo. The visitor center museum features both Indian and Spanish colonial artifacts.

Area Attractions

While visiting the area, why not plan a trip to Rio Grande Nature Center State Park? This day-use park is located at the end of Candelaria Road, west of Interstate 25 in Albuquerque. Situated on the Rio Grande, the park is winter home to Canada geese, sandhill cranes and other waterfowl. Trails, nature viewing areas and a library complement the extensive visitor center exhibits.

For further information contact the Park Superintendent, Coronado State Park, Barnalillo, NM 87128. ☎ (505) 867-5589.

Fenton Lake State Park

Location: 33 miles northwest of San Ysidro via NM 4.

A popular year-round retreat surrounded by beautiful ponderosa pine forests, the park features a cross-country ski and biathlon trail and wheelchair-accessible fishing platforms.

For further information contact the Park Superintendent, ☎ (505) 829-3630.

Manzano Mountains State Park

Location: 13 miles northwest of Mountainair via NM 55.

Nestled in the wooded foothills of the Manzano Mountains, the park is an excellent place for birdwatching, photography, hiking, and cross-country skiing. Salinas National Monument is located nearby.

For further information contact the Park Superintent, Manzano Mountains State Park, Mountainair, NM 87038. ☎ (505) 847-2820.

Rio Grande Nature Center

Location: In Albuquerque on Candelaria northwest.

This park features 270 acres of riverside forest and meadows which include stands of 100-year-old cottonwoods, clumps of willow, tamarisk and Russian olive, and a cattail marsh alongside a three-acre pond.

The bosque, as this area is called in the Southwest, is threaded with two miles of nature trails, offering a sense of isolation and tranquility as they wind through partially wooded areas to open sand flats alongside the Rio Grande River.

Over 260 species of birds have made this their home. Watch for sandhill cranes. Over 21 interpretive exhibits inform you of the natural, historical and social implications of the Rio Grande River.

For further information contact the Park Superintendent, Rio Grande Nature Center, 2901 Candelaria N.W., Albuquerque, NM 87107. ☎ (505) 344-7240.

Senator Willie M. Chavez State Park

Location: In Belen on E. River Road.

Birdwatching and hiking are popular with visitors to this park, located in the cottonwoods along the Rio Grande.

For further information contact the Park Superintendent, Senator Willie M. Chavez State Park, NM 87002. ☎ (505) 864-3915.

Chaco Canyon National Historic Park

From Gallup: exit I-40 at Thoreau (Exit 53) and go north on NM 371, two miles north on Crownpoint, and turn east on NM 57. After 15 miles, turn north at the marked turnoff and drive 20 miles to the visitor center.
From Grants: take Exit 79 off of I-40 and travel north on NM 509 (initially called NM 605) for about 53 miles. At White Horse, turn west of NM 57 and drive another 10 miles to the Chaco Canyon turnoff. The visitor center is 20 miles on a dirt road.

Reaching the park can be tricky, because the dirt roads that lead to it are sometimes impassable. Contact the visitor center for current conditions.

History

The ruins of Chaco Canyon are a window into the Southwest's ancient and glorious past. More than 600 years ago, the arid canyon was home to over 400 settlements and a hub for many more. Archeologists have found evidence of ancient roads that link Chaco Canyon to about 70 villages scattered throughout the region, including Mesa Verde, 90 miles northwest.

The Ruins of Bonito are a testament to the technological advancement of the culture. Covering more than three acres, Bonito contained about 600 rooms and more than 30 kivas. As many as 1,200 people could have lived inside its four-story walls.

Even the masonry of the building suggests a high level of skill. The Chacoans cut stones of different sizes to fit together perfectly inside smooth, straight walls. They even made the bases of their walls thicker to support future additions above.

The canyon is an endless source of mystery for archeologists and a fascinating adventure for laymen. The park has a dozen ruins that invite even the first-time explorer to ask questions. How did the Chacoans bring water to this arid land? How did they keep control over such a large region? And, most importantly, why did they disappear in the 12th century?

About eight ruins have been excavated for viewing along a seven-mile paved route. Those with more time can also camp in the park and hike to an additional five sites scattered nearby.

Facilities

Park facilities include a visitor center, campground, and picnic sites. Camping is limited to 14 days, and trailers longer than 30 feet cannot be accommodated. The visitor center is the park's only source of potable water.

For more information the Site Superintendent, Chaco Canyon National Monument, c/o National Park Service, PO Box 728, Santa Fe, NM 87504-0728. ☎ (505) 988-6716 or (505) 988-6727.

National Parks

Carlsbad Caverns National Park

Location: North on I-80 to White's City.

Your encounter with Carlsbad Caverns National Park begins in the Chihuahuan Desert of the Guadalupe Mountains. But beyond the somewhat familiar surroundings of rugged mountains and broad plains is another world. Away from the sunlight, away from the flowering cactus, away from the songs of the desert birds and the howl of the coyote, lies the celebrated underground world of Carlsbad Cavern. It is an incomparable realm of gigantic subterranean chambers, fantastic cave formations, and extraordinary features. The first adventurers entering Carlsbad Cavern had no idea what to expect as they walked, crawled, and climbed down into the darkness. Today many of the wonders of Carlsbad Cavern are well know, yet the experience of exploring its chambers is every bit as exciting as it was to the first adventurers.

The park's climate is characterized by warm summers and mild winters. In the summer average highs are in the 90°F, in the winter they are in the 50s and 60s. Intense thunderstorms occur in the summer, posing the danger of lightning in higher areas and of floods in low-lying areas.

History

More than 1,000 years ago prehistoric Indians ventured into Carlsbad Cavern seeking shelter. They left no record of what their impressions of the cave were, but they did leave some mysterious drawings on cave walls near the natural entrance. Much later, in the 1800s, settlers discovered the cavern, drawn to it by the spectacle of hundreds of thousands of bats rising up out of the natural entrance in the evening. Some stayed to mine the huge deposits of bat guano in the cave and sell it as a natural fertilizer. One such man, a cowboy named Jim White, became fascinated by the cave and spent days exploring it. White was eager to show the many natural wonders of this extraordinary place to others, but few persons believed his improbable tales of a huge underground wilderness full of unusual cave formations. It took photographs to convince skeptics that Carlsbad Caverns was everything it was said to be, and more. Black and white pictures taken by Ray V. Davis, who accompanied White on a cave trip, were displayed in the town of Carlsbad in 1915. They created a sensation. People suddenly clamored to see the marvelous cave for themselves. White took them on tours that began with an unceremonious 170-foot descent in a bucket once used to haul bat guano from the cave.

Word of the cave spread, finally reaching Washington, D.C. Again, there were nonbelievers but, in 1923, the US Department of the Interior sent inspector Robert Holley to investigate and see whether Carlsbad Cavern was truly an outstanding natural scenic wonder. Originally a skeptic, Holly wrote in his final report: "I am wholly conscious of the feebleness of my efforts to convey in words the deep conflicting emotions, the feeling of fear and awe, and the desire for an inspired understanding of the Divine Creator's work which presents to the human eye such a complex aggregate of natural wonders."

Later that year Carlsbad Cavern was proclaimed a national monument. White, who was to continue his cave explorations for most of his lifetime, became its first chief ranger. Seven years later, Carlsbad Caverns National Park was created to protect the cave. Through illustrated articles published in magazines such as *National Geographic* and by word of mouth, Carlsbad Cavern became on of the world's most celebrated caves. Since its establishment, the park has been expanded in size and today includes 46,755 acres and more than 70 other smaller caves.

And the exploration of Carlsbad Cavern continues. Experienced underground explorers, or cavers, and cave scientists are the Christopher Columbuses of today, journeying beyond the boundaries of what is known into the realm of the unknown. Carlsbad Cavern attracts many men and women who are eager to shed light on some of its mysteries. Teams of cavers well versed in safe exploration techniques continue to discover new portions of the cave. Their finds in recent years include the Guadalupe Room, Carlsbad Cavern's second largest room, in 1966; the exceptionally colorful and much-decorated Bifrost Room, in 1982, and the Rim Room, one of the most recent discoveries, in 1984.

How the Caves were Formed

Carlsbad Cavern began 250 million years ago with the creation of a 400-mile-long reef in an inland sea that covered this region. This horseshoe-shaped reef was formed from the remains of sponges, algae, and seashells. Eventually the sea evaporated and the reef was buried under deposits of salts and gypsum. Then, a few million years ago, uplift and erosion of the area began to uncover the buried rock reef. Rainwater, made slightly acidic from the air and soil, seeped down into the cracks in the reef, slowly dissolving the limestone and beginning the process that would form large underground chambers. Many geologists believe that the fresh rainwater mixed with deeper salty water to form sulfuric acid. The added power of this very corrosive substance could explain the tremendous size of the passageways. The exposed reef became a part of the Guadalupe Mountains and the huge underground chambers far below the surface became the natural wonder of Carlsbad Cavern.

The decoration of Carlsbad Cavern with stalactites, stalagmites, and an incredible variety of other formations began more than 500,000 years ago after much of the cavern had been carved out. It happened slowly, drop by drop, at a time when a wetter, cooler climate prevailed. The creation of each formation depended on water that dripped or seeped down through the limestone bedrock. As a raindrop fell to the ground and percolated downward, it absorbed carbon dioxide from the air and soil, and a weak acid was formed. As it continued to move downward the drop dissolved a little limestone, absorbing a bit of the basic ingredient needed to build most cave formations – the mineral calcite. Once the drop finally emerged in the cave, the carbon dioxide escaped into the cave air. No longer able to hold the dissolved calcite, the drop deposited its tiny mineral load as a crystal of calcite. Billions and billions of drops later, an amazing array of shapes had been formed. Where water dripped slowly from the ceiling, soda straws and larger stalactites appeared. Water falling on the floor created stalagmites. Sometimes a stalactite and stalagmite joined, forming a column. Draperies were hung where water ran down a slanted ceiling. Water flowing over the surface of a wall or floor deposited layers of calcite called flowstone. Cave pearls, lily pads, and rimstone dams appeared where pools of water or streams occurred in the cave. Like oyster pearls, cave pearls were made as layer upon layer of calcite built up around a grain of sand or other tiny object. Lily pads formed on the surface of pools, while dams formed where water flowed slowly on the floor. Another type of cave formation that decorated cave walls was popcorn, which may have formed when water evaporated and left behind calcite deposits. Some of the more unusual formations are helictites, which grow seemingly without regard to gravity, their twisting shapes governed by crystal shapes, impurities, and the force of water under pressure. Other rare formations are those composed not of calcite, but of aragonite, a mineral chemically identical to calcite, but with a different crystal structure. These formations tend to be small, delicate, and needle-like.

The Bats

As many as seven types of bats may roost in Carlsbad Cavern, but none is as prevalent as the Mexican free-tail. Gray or sometimes brown, this bat is distinguished by its long, narrow wings and a dangling, skinny tail. Like most species of bats, Mexican free-tails navigate and locate their prey by emitting ultra-high frequency sounds. Known as echolocation, this natural sonar system is similar to that used by dolphins and whales. When a bat's signals strike an object, they are reflected back and heard by the bat. The bat then takes whatever action is appropriate, whether it be zeroing in on a tiny moth or swerving to avoid a tree limb.

Carlsbad Caverns is a sanctuary for about 300,000 Mexican free-tail bats. During the day they crowd together on the ceiling of Bat Cave, a passageway near the natural entrance of Carlsbad Cavern. In this darkened home they are seen only by researchers. At night-fall, however, the bats leave the cave in gigantic swarms.

The evening flight of the bats of Carlsbad Cavern is a natural phenomenon as fascinating as the cave itself. In a mass exodus at dusk, thousands of Mexican free-tail bats fly from the cave for a night of feasting on insects. The spectacle can be viewed from the outdoor amphitheater at the cave's natural entrance. Before each flight a park ranger gives a short talk on bats; check at the visitor center for the schedule. Because the bats winter in Mexico, the flights occur only from early spring through October. The spectacular night flight begins with a few bats. Then, in a matter of minutes, a thick whirlwind of bats spirals out of the cave up into the darkening night sky. The exodus can last 20 minutes or as long as 2½ hours. Once out of the cave, the undulating mass of thousands of bats flies, in serpentine fashion, southeast to feed in the Pecos and Black River valleys. Once there, they begin gorging themselves on moths and other night-flying insects. Each bat may eat several stomachfuls in a single night. With the coming of dawn, the bats begin flying back to the cave individually or in small groups. They reenter the cave in a fashion almost as remarkable as their departure. Each bat positions itself high above the cave entrance. It then folds its wings close to its body, and plummets like a hailstone into the blackness of Carlsbad Cavern, making a strange buzzing sound as it does. One by one, the bats return to the safety of the Bat Cave, where they sleep until emerging in the dusk of the next day. Silhouetted against the night sky like a dark, swift-moving cloud, the bats make their most dramatic display.

The Bat Cave serves as a warm-weather home, as a daytime refuge and, perhaps most importantly, as a maternity roost for the bats. Under cover of darkness, away from the predators or disturbances, the young are born in June. A female usually has just one offspring. Each birth occurs on the ceiling as the mother hangs by her toes and thumbs. For the next four to five weeks the youngster remains on the ceiling. During the day mother and young hang in clusters, resting, napping, and nursing. As many as 300 bats may crowd into one square foot. At night, the young are left in the cave while the adults leave to feed. In July or August, each young bat takes its first flight, joining the adults on nightly feeding forays.

Touring the Caves

Explore the vast underground world of Carlsbad Cavern along two tour routes. The routes – designated the Blue Tour and the Red Tour – both follow paved, well lighted trails. Exhibits are located along the trails, and park rangers are there to answer questions and give assistance. Underground facilities are limited to restrooms and the Underground Lunchroom. Begin your tour at the visitor center, where entrance fees are collected and up-to-date information on the cave are available.

The cave is open every day of the year except December 25th. Hours vary; a current schedule is posted at the center. During most of the year you can walk the Blue Tour on your own. However, the first half of this tour is ranger-guided the first two weeks in December, most of January, and the first part of February. The Red Tour is self-guided all year.

On the three-mile **Blue Tour** you see all the chambers of Carlsbad Cavern that are open to the public – the Main Corridor, the Scenic Rooms, and the Big Room. The tour takes 2½ to 3 hours. The route is strenuous and is not recommended for persons with walking, breathing, or heart problems.

The Blue Tour begins at the visitor center and goes through the cave's natural entrance. Once you leave behind the area illuminated by sunlight, you begin your descent into the Main Corridor. This steeply descending passageway is not greatly decorated with cave formations, but its size – more than a quarter-mile long with ceiling heights of more than 200 feet – is staggering. Equally impressive is the depth to which it takes you – 829 feet below the surface. The scattered decorations in the Main Corridor include stalactites, stalagmites, and flowstone. At the end of the Main Corridor lies Iceberg Rock, a 200,000-ton boulder that fell from the ceiling thousands of years ago.

From the Main Corridor you step into the smaller Scenic Rooms. The first is the Green Lake Room, a wonderland of thousands of delicate stalactites, marble-like flowstone, and eight-foot-deep Green Lake. From this chamber you continue into the rest of the exquisitely decorated Scenic Rooms – the Kings Palace, the Queens Chamber, and the Papoose Room. The trail then ascends to the Boneyard, an undecorated area that may resemble what Carlsbad Cavern looked like during earlier years.

Nearby is the Underground Lunchroom, where you can rest and have a light meal. The cave's only restrooms are located here. When you resume your tour you will continue into the Big Room, the grand finale (see description under "Red Tour," below).

The 1¼-mile **Red Tour** explores the immense subterranean chamber called, appropriately, the Big Room. The tour takes 1 to 1½ hours. Most of the route is fairly level and accessible to wheelchairs.

The Red Tour begins with a minute-long elevator ride 755 feet down from the visitor center to the edge of the Big Room. (Persons following the Blue Tour route merely have to walk from the Underground Lunchroom into the Big Room.) A cross-shaped room, the Big Room measures 1,800 feet at its longest, 1,100 feet at its widest, and 255 feet at its highest. It is one of the largest underground chambers in the world. The tour takes you along the perimeter of the room so you can experience every corner of this extraordinary place. From bottom to top and from side to side, this chamber is resplendent with cave formations, including the 62-foot-high Giant Dome, Carlsbad's biggest stalagmite, and the 42-foot-high Twin Domes in the Hall of Giants, as well as numerous other stalagmites, stalactites, columns, draperies, and flowstone formations. Some other highlights of the tour are crystal clear Mirror Lake and the Bottomless Pit, a black hole 140 feet deep. Park rangers give talks about the cave at the seating area near the Top of the Cross. After circling the Big Room you return to the surface by elevator.

Other Park Activities

The visitor center has a variety of information on all features of the park, including the mountains and desert. Books, brochures, a topographic dimensional model of Carlsbad Cavern and park activity schedules are available. Park rangers can assist you in planning what to see and do both on the surface and underground. There's also a restaurant, gift shop, nursery, and kennel at the center. All services are available year-round, except on Christmas Day.

The 9½-mile Walnut Canyon Desert Drive is a gravel, one-way loop through dramatic desert mountain scenery. Passenger cars can travel the road easily, but the narrow, twisting route is not recommended for trailers or motor homes. A guide booklet is available at the visitor center.

Hiking

The park's trail system includes a short nature trail and, for experienced hikers, more than 50 miles of primitive backcountry trails. Trailheads are located along each of the park roads. Backcountry hikers should register at the visitor center. A good supply of water and a topographic map are essential.

Camping and Picnicking

There is no developed campground in the park, but the nearby towns of White's City and Carlsbad have several. (These towns also have lodging, restaurants, gasoline stations, and other services.) Free backcountry permits are available at the visitor center. Picnic tables are located near the visitor center and in Walnut Canyon. Rattlesnake Springs has a picnic area with tables, grills, drinking water, and restrooms.

Slaughter Canyon Cave

Ranger-guided tours of Slaughter Canyon Cave take you into an underground wilderness without electricity, paved walkways, or other modern conveniences. In this wild cave, darkness is broken only by the light of lanterns carried by rangers and flashlights carried by tour members. Among the highlights of the two-hour, 1¼-mile tour are the 89-foot Monarch, one of the world's tallest columns; the sparkling, crystal-decorated Christmas Tree column; and the Chinese Wall, a delicate, ankle-high rimstone dam. Old bat guano mining excavations can also be seen. Tours are given daily in the summer and on weekends the rest of the year. A fee is charged. Reservations must be made at the visitor center or by calling the park. You have to hike a strenuous half-mile to reach the cave entrance, where the tour begins. Sturdy walking shoes, flashlights, and water are required.

For more information, ☎ (505) 785-2232; or write Superintendent, Carlsbad Caverns National Park, 3225 National Parks Highway, Carlsbad, NM 88220.